Practical Microsoft Azure IaaS

Migrating and Building Scalable and Secure Cloud Solutions

Shijimol Ambi Karthikeyan

Apress®

Practical Microsoft Azure IaaS

Shijimol Ambi Karthikeyan
Bangalore, Karnataka, India

ISBN-13 (pbk): 978-1-4842-3762-5   ISBN-13 (electronic): 978-1-4842-3763-2
https://doi.org/10.1007/978-1-4842-3763-2

Library of Congress Control Number: 2018951267

Managing Director, Apress Media LLC: Welmoed Spahr
Acquisitions Editor: Smriti Srivastava
Development Editor: Matthew Moodie
Coordinating Editor: Shrikant Vishwakarma

Cover designed by eStudioCalamar

Cover image designed by Freepik (www.freepik.com)

Distributed to the book trade worldwide by Springer Science+Business Media New York, 233 Spring Street, 6th Floor, New York, NY 10013. Phone 1-800-SPRINGER, fax (201) 348-4505, e-mail orders-ny@springer-sbm.com, or visit www.springeronline.com. Apress Media, LLC is a California LLC and the sole member (owner) is Springer Science + Business Media Finance Inc (SSBM Finance Inc). SSBM Finance Inc is a **Delaware** corporation.

For information on translations, please e-mail rights@apress.com, or visit http://www.apress.com/rights-permissions.

Apress titles may be purchased in bulk for academic, corporate, or promotional use. eBook versions and licenses are also available for most titles. For more information, reference our Print and eBook Bulk Sales web page at http://www.apress.com/bulk-sales.

Any source code or other supplementary material referenced by the author in this book is available to readers on GitHub via the book's product page, located at www.apress.com/978-1-4842-3762-5. For more detailed information, please visit http://www.apress.com/source-code.

Printed on acid-free paper

Dedicated to my dearest Amma and Achan,
my guardian angels watching over me from heaven....

Table of Contents

About the Author

Shijimol Ambi Karthikeyan currently works as a cloud consultant with Microsoft. She has more than 12 years of experience in IT and specializes in datacenter management, virtualization, and cloud computing technologies. She started her career with EY IT services on the datacenter management team, where she managed complex virtualized production datacenters. She has expertise in managing VMware and Hyper-V virtualization stacks and Windows/Linux server technologies.

Shijimol has also worked on DevOps CI/CD implementation projects using tools like TeamCity, Jenkins, Git, TortoiseSVN, Mercurial, Selenium, and so forth. She later moved on to cloud computing and gained expertise in Windows Azure, focusing on Azure IaaS, backup, disaster recovery, and automation.

Shijimol holds industry standard certifications in technologies such as Microsoft Azure, Windows Server, and VMware. She also holds ITIL and TOGAF 9 certifications. She has also authored *Azure Automation Using the ARM Model* (Apress, 2017).

About the Technical Reviewer

Kapil Bansal is a technical consultant at HCL Technologies in India. He has more than ten years of experience in the IT industry. He has worked on Microsoft Azure cloud computing (PaaS and IaaS), Azure Stack, DevOps, release management, ALM, ITIL, and Six Sigma. He has worked with companies such as IBM India Private Ltd., NIIT Technologies, Encore Capital Group, and Xavient Software Solutions, and he has served clients based in the United States, the United Kingdom, India, and Africa, including T-Mobile, WBMI, Encore Capital, and Bharti Airtel.

Acknowledgments

First and foremost, I would like to thank my parents for everything that I have ever accomplished in my life, including this book. My mother, Ambi R., always inspired me to work toward my goals no matter how unrealistic others perceive them to be. My father, Karthikeyan M., taught me that it is equally important to slow down at times and take in life as it is. They are no longer around, but their love and blessings keep me going.

My husband, Sujai Sugathan, supported me throughout this endeavor like he always does for all my adventures. My daughter, Sanjana Sujai, the sweetheart she is, gracefully put up with my absenteeism while I was busy authoring the book. I am grateful for the support I get from my sister, Gigimol A. K., and family; my in-laws; and my extended family. I would also like to thank my best friend, Anjana, for her unwavering confidence in me. I am thankful to the mentors in my professional life (there are too many to name) for their constant support and encouragement. Last but not least, I would like to thank the entire team at Apress for their support during the publishing process.

Introduction

Infrastructure as a service (IaaS) is the most common cloud deployment model, and it is most preferred by enterprises adopting a hybrid cloud strategy. This book is designed to be a hands-on guide for organizations planning to adopt Azure IaaS and to migrate their on-premise infrastructure partially or fully to Azure. The important design factors to be considered during this process are explained in this book, starting from assessment, planning, identifying, and mapping services and best practice implementations.

Chapter 1 introduces the basic compute, storage, and networking components in Azure IaaS.

Chapter 2 explores the different options available for migrating compute workloads from on-premise datacenters hosted in physical or virtualization platforms like VMware and Hyper-V.

Chapter 3 covers Azure IaaS storage and network components and configuration scenarios during migration.

Chapter 4 focuses on the different options available to build environments at scale in Azure.

Chapter 5 explains how to build resilient environments in Azure by leveraging various platform components.

Chapter 6 discusses deploying highly available environments in Azure using features and tools such as availability sets, load balancers, and application gateways.

Chapter 7 showcases some of the monitoring and automation tools available in Azure to optimize deployments.

Chapter 8 explains Azure security best practices and provides a walkthrough of the different security configurations at platform level and resource level.

Chapter 9 focuses on sample IaaS architectures and related implementation best practices.

CHAPTER 1

Introduction to Azure IaaS

Since the dawn of public clouds, vast pools of compute, storage, and networking resources are now available and at the disposal of users who want to leverage them on a pay-as-you-go basis. The ease of implementation and usage becomes one of the key differentiators for organizations while they select their preferred cloud service provider. Built on top of reliable Microsoft server and virtualization technologies, Azure accelerates the adoption journey of enterprises, whether they are interested in purely cloud-based environments or in a hybrid setup.

Infrastructure as a service (IaaS) is usually the first step for any organization planning to move from legacy on-premise systems to the cloud. Changing from traditional on-premise design standards to the more evolved and complex Microsoft Azure cloud standards can be daunting for infrastructure architects. Design practicality and adherence to stringent design guidelines should be kept in mind. Selecting the right resource types lays the foundation of an IaaS architecture. This chapter helps with building this foundation and introduces the basic components of Azure IaaS.

© Shijimol Ambi Karthikeyan 2018
S. Ambi Karthikeyan, *Practical Microsoft Azure IaaS*,
https://doi.org/10.1007/978-1-4842-3763-2_1

What's New in Azure Resource Manager (ARM Model)

There are two deployment models available in Azure: classic and Azure Resource Manager (ARM). The first one was a monolithic deployment model with little or no flexibility to group together or manage resources in a subscription. It followed a flat structure in terms of identity and access management; the co-admin role provided at the subscription level had full access to all resources. The Azure Resource Manager model (ARM) was introduced in 2014 and brought several enhancements over the classic model.

Let's look at some of the key changes introduced with the ARM architecture.

Resource Groups

Resource groups are logical containers used to group resources that share the same lifecycle. Entities that were interdependent or related are now managed as a single unit in terms of deployment, access control, and so forth.

JSON–Based ARM Templates

JavaScript Object Notation (JSON)–based ARM templates brought in a new revolution in automation. Multitiered applications and their dependencies are easily deployed using ARM templates. The public ARM repository holds templates contributed by the community, as well as Microsoft product teams, which cover most of the common deployment use cases. If not, users can easily tweak the available templates to meet their requirements.

Role-Based Access Control

Role-based access control (RBAC) replaces the flat identity structure of the classic model. RBAC provides fine-grained access control to resources deployed using ARM. The basic roles are owner, contributor, and reader. The owner role has full access to all resources in the assigned scope; for example, users that are assigned the owner role of the subscription have full access to all resources in the subscription. (You can also give other users access to the subscription.)

The contributor role also has full access at the assigned scope; however, you cannot give other users access to the assigned scope. The reader role has only read access to resources. Other than the basic roles, there are built-in roles that provide specific access to resources; for example, backup operator and backup reader roles only provide access in the scope of backup services. You can also create your own custom roles if none of the built-in roles meets your requirements.

IaaS Compute Services

Compute services form the backbone of any infrastructure, whether on-premise or in the cloud. When it comes to hosting environments on-premise, the scalability of compute resources is a major challenge. It is this problem, along with many others, that IaaS is trying to resolve. Microsoft Azure provides a variety of compute offerings that cater to multiple workload types and use cases. Let's start by learning about the features and use cases of the major Azure IaaS compute components.

Virtual Machines

Virtual machines (VMs) are the basic building blocks of Azure IaaS compute. Considering the great number of workloads being migrated to Microsoft Azure, there are many VM instance types or SKUs to choose from.

VM Pricing Tiers

Before we take a deep dive into the instance types/SKUs, let's look at the three VM pricing tiers: basic, standard, and low-priority.

Basic Tier

The basic tier VMs are for non-production workloads largely targeting test/dev environments or crash-and-burn scenarios. Although you can put VMs in availability sets, you cannot connect them to a load balancer to ensure high availability. The number of instance types available under this tier is limited. Moreover, these instances do not support SSD-based hard disks for improved disk performance. Typically, organizations getting started with Azure prefer this tier for the initial testing phase, after which they can be upgraded to the standard tier.

Standard Tier

The standard tier is for production workloads. It supports all production-ready features, such as load balancing, solid-state drive (SSD) hard disks, and so forth. It also provides a wide variety of VM instance types. The standard tier supports specialized workloads that need memory/CPU/storage intensive VMs or VMs with graphical cards.

Low-Priority Tier

The low-priority tier is the latest addition to the VM pricing tier, but it is not used in simple, independent VM deployments. Low-priority VMs are currently supported only in Azure batch services, where tasks are executed asynchronously by a large group of computers. Low-priority VMs are part of this group. They are allocated whenever available and pre-empted when the compute power is required by high-priority workloads. However, the choice to use low-priority VMs can significantly reduce the associated compute costs.

Azure Compute Unit (ACU)

Azure compute units (ACU) define the compute power available to a VM. The ACU baseline is 100, which is the compute power of Standard_A1 SKU. ACUs of other instance types are measured with reference to that of Standard_A1. The current list of VM instance types and their ACUs are listed in Table 1-1.

Table 1-1. VM Instance Types and Their ACUs

VM Instance Type/SKU Family	ACU
A0	50
A1–A4	100
A5–A7	100
A1_v2–A8_v2	100
A2m_v2–A8m_v2	100
A8–A11	225
D1–D14	160
D1_v2–D15_v2	210–250
DS1–DS14	160
DS1_v2–DS15_v2	210–250
D_v3	160–190
Ds_v3	160–190
E_v3	160–190
Es_v3	160–190
F2s_v2–F72s_v2	195–210
F1–F16	210–250
F1s–F16s	210–250
G1–G5	180 – 240
GS1–GS5	180 – 240
H	290 – 300
L4s–L32s	180 – 240
M	160–180

All instance types except A0–A7, A1_V2-A8_V2, A2m_V2-A8m_V2, D1-D14, and DS1-DS14 use Intel Turbo Boost Technology to increase CPU performance.

VM Instance Types/SKUs

VM instance types are categorized by the targeted workloads. More instance types have been added to this portfolio based on customer demand. As of this writing, the following VM instance types are available in Azure.

- **General purpose**. These are VMs from instance types A to D, suited for generic workloads and dev/test environments. Among these SKUs, the D series provides better CPU performance than the A series. DV2 and DV3 are next-generation VMs to the original D series and can provide up to 35% more CPU performance than their predecessors. The B series provide burstable VMs. When the VM utilizes fewer resources, credits are accumulated, which are later used to utilize more CPU whenever there is a requirement for higher CPU performance.

- **Compute optimized**. These SKUs are ideal for workloads that need optimum compute capacity, such as network appliances and application servers. F, FS, and FS_V2 machines fall under this category. Machines in the F series are ideal for compute-intensive applications but have minimal memory and temporary storage per vCPU requirements.

- **Memory optimized**. These SKUs are for memory-intensive applications with high memory-to-CPU ratio requirements. The M series machines in this SKU offer instance types with memory as high as 3.8 TB, which can be used in large relational databases.

7

- **Storage optimized**. Workloads that need high storage IOPS (input/output operations per second) requirements benefit from this SKU. The L series machines can have maximum of 32 vCPUs, 256 GB of memory, and 64 TB of storage for the largest instance type available (i.e., the Standard_L32s series).

- **GPU**. Azure offers VMs with NVIDIA GPUs under the N series. There are three variants of VMs in this SKU: NC, ND, and NV. They are differentiated by GPUs. The NC series uses a NVIDIA TESLA K80 card, NCv2 uses NVIDIA TESLA P100, ND uses NVIDIA Tesla P40 GPUs, and the NV series uses NVIDIA Tesla M60 GPUs.

- **High-performance compute**. These SKUs target compute and network-intensive high-performance compute applications. The use cases are advanced modeling, clusters, and simulations. Instances A8–A11 and H series machines fall under this category. H series machines also feature DDR4 memory and SSD-based temporary storage.

VM Deployment Considerations

The following considerations are applicable for all VMs at the planning phase, irrespective of VM instance type.

- The availability of VMs in each geographical region is not always guaranteed. You need to check the Azure services availability matrix to confirm that the instance type that you are planning to use is available in that geographical region.

- The number of additional data disks that can be attached to a VM is dependent on the type of VM selected. If you need a VM of higher capacity, you can change to an instance type that supports more data disks.

- The memory and CPU cores available with a specific instance type are fixed. There is no option to increase or reduce the memory or core of a given instance type. You need to either scale up or scale down to an instance type that supports the required compute capacity.

- When VMs are initially deployed, you can choose them to be part of an existing or new availability set to ensure high availability. It is not possible to change this selection after VM deployment without deleting and re-creating the VM. Refer to Chapter 5 of this book for more information on availability sets.

- Only VM instance types with the "s" suffix support premium storage or SSD-based disks, such as DS2v2, F2S, B2S, and so forth. After VM deployment, if there is a requirement to add SSD, you first need to change the VM instance type to either of these VMs instance types with the "s" suffix so that the premium disk can be added.

Getting Started with VM Creation

Creating virtual machines from the Azure portal can be done quite easily in a few steps.

In the Azure portal, click **Create a resource ➤ Compute**. Select the OS image from the Azure Marketplace, as shown in Figure 1-1.

Figure 1-1. *Create a new VM*

Enter the basic VM configuration settings, such as name, disk type, username, and password. Select the resource group (use an existing one or create a new one) and the location, as shown in Figure 1-2. If you have an existing license with software assurance enabled, you can leverage the Azure hybrid benefit and save on VM costs.

Figure 1-2. *VM basic settings*

Next, choose the right VM size. By default, a set of recommended VM sizes are listed, as shown in Figure 1-3. Click **View all** to see the available instance types in the given region, and select the correct instance type.

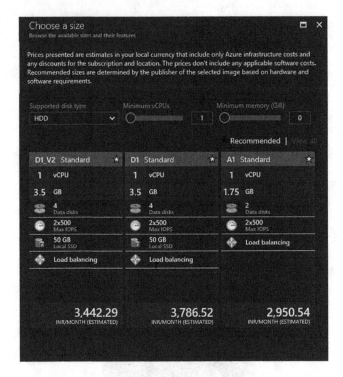

Figure 1-3. *Recommended VM instance types*

In the next step, the following important and mandatory settings are configured (see Figure 1-4).

- **Availability sets**. It is recommended to group production VMs into availability sets. This should be done during VM provisioning, because changing the availability set after VM creation is not possible.

- **Managed disks**. You have the option to use managed disks. Additional storage configuration is not required if you use managed disks. (Managed disks are discussed in detail later in this chapter).

- **Storage** and **Network**. If you are using unmanaged
  disks, configure where the disks will be stored. Any
  existing storage in the same subscription and region
  is listed. You can either select existing storage or
  create new storage. This also applies to networks. You
  select an existing or new virtual network, the subnet,
  public IP, and network security group. If you do not
  select an existing network security group, a new
  network security group is created and default rules are
  added. For Windows VMs, incoming Remote Desktop
  Protocol (RDP) traffic is allowed by default. For Linux,
  SSH traffic is allowed in the new network security
  group (NSG).

Figure 1-4. VM storage, availability, and network settings

Additionally, you can choose to enable VM extensions, which are agent-like applications that are installed in VMs during post deployment to carry specific functionalities, such as anti-malware protection, DSC configuration, and so forth.

If you are running a dev or test environment, you might want to shut down your machines after office hours by using the Auto Shutdown settings. The monitoring settings can be configured to capture boot diagnostics and guest OS diagnostics. You can also enable regular backup of the VMs to be stored in a new or existing Azure Recovery Services vault.

Once all the settings are configured, review the summary and click the Create button to create the VM.

Now let's explore a few more compute options in Azure IaaS.

Virtual Machine Scale Sets (VMSS)

Virtual Machine Scale Sets (VMSS) are Azure compute resources that provide horizontal autoscaling of hosted applications depending on defined performance metrics like CPU, memory utilization, and disk I/O. Integrating scale sets into the architecture automatically takes care of peak-hour resources surge requirements. Whenever the resource utilization is below the defined threshold, VMSS automatically scales and reduces the number of deployed VMs. Take into consideration, however, that hosted applications should natively support horizontal scaling. The platform simply spins up additional VMs using the designated image once the scaling thresholds are triggered.

Autoscaling in VMSS

Autoscaling methods can be configured with VMSS. They are leveraged based on the architecture and use case requirements.

Autoscaling metrics include the default host-based ones available without any additional configuration, in-guest metrics made available by installing the Azure diagnostics extension, and application-level metrics using Application Insights.

The following host-based metrics can be leveraged to create autoscaling rules:

- CPU utilization percentage

- Network in/out

- Disk read/write bytes

- Disk read/write operations per second

- CPU credits remaining/consumed

In-guest metrics need the Azure diagnostics extension to be installed on the VM, which stores diagnostics data to a storage account. The advantage is the availability of fine-grained metrics, such as information from OS performance counters, to trigger autoscaling. Application Insights is a service that provides performance insights into your application. You can create autoscaling rules in VM scale sets using the application metrics information made available by Application Insights.

VMSS Use Cases and Design Considerations

VMSS may not be suitable for all applications, specifically ones that need to store static data. The service targets stateless applications designed to work for distributed processing. This includes scenarios where you want to provide a static web front end to your customers, while the data handling is taken care of by a persistent back-end tier.

The required level of scaling is another factor to consider. If you are planning to use custom images, you cannot have more than 300 VMs in a single scale set. This restriction is not applicable for scale sets using marketplace images that can scale up to 1000 VMs. In a real-world application scenario, however, you might want to make customizations to the image so that the VMs are plugged in and functional as soon as they are up and running.

If you need scaling in the range of 1000 VMs with customization requirements, you can still use an Azure Marketplace image and then use a post-deployment custom script execution. This can be done using the custom script extension or the PowerShell DSC extension. Custom script extensions can be used to execute scripts for installing required applications by using PowerShell scripts downloaded to the deployed VMs from an Azure Storage blob. PowerShell DSC extensions leverage DSC and enforce specific configurations to deployed VMs.

It is recommended to use managed disks wherever possible with VMSS wherever possible because the storage management overhead is handled by the platform. There are limitations to using user-managed storages with VMSS because Azure's storage limits, such as VMs per storage and disk I/O, come into picture. The number of VMs allowed in VMSS using user-managed storage is limited to 100.

VMSS scalability features are further discussed in Chapter 3.

DevTest Labs

Azure DevTest Labs set up development and test environments targeting fail-fast or crash-and-burn scenarios. DevTest Labs provide additional control over the cloud resources used for development and testing, while maintaining the flexibility of a self-service model. DevTest Labs consist of several components, including virtual machines, images, artifacts, artifact repositories, policies, and quotas.

Features and Provisioning

The easiest way to create a new DevTest Lab is from the Azure portal. Click **All services** and search for "devtest" (see Figure 1-5).

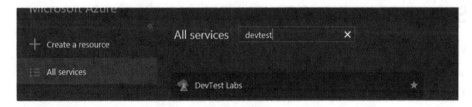

Figure 1-5. Select DevTest Labs in the Azure portal

Provide basic details—such as name, subscription, location, and tags—to create the DevTest Lab, as shown in Figure 1-6.

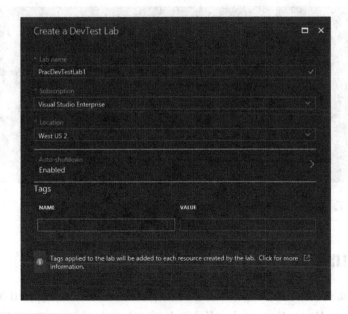

Figure 1-6. DevTest Labs basic settings

The lab is created in a new resource group. You can now add any new VMs to the lab. Now let's take a look at few basic settings and policies in this lab.

Secure Storage of Credentials

You can add all usernames and passwords, SSH public keys, or GitHub access tokens in the DevTest Labs My Secrets store, as shown in Figure 1-7. This is a key vault created for each user for secure storage of credentials. Navigate to **My secrets** in the left pane of the newly created DevTest Lab. Add the name value pair and click Save. As seen in Figure 1-7, the value/ password is encrypted and stored. Once created, it cannot be edited; the user has to delete it and create it again to make any updates.

Figure 1-7. DevTest Labs "My secrets" option

Configuration and Policies

All policies, settings, and quotas related to a lab can be configured by selecting **Configuration and policies**. Let's take a look at some of the important settings that should be configured for optimal utilization of the DevTest Labs service.

- **Allowed VM sizes.** If you enable the allowed VM sizes option, the administrator has the capability to restrict the VM sizes available for users, as shown in Figure 1-8.

Figure 1-8. *Allowed VM sizes*

- **Virtual machines per user**. This setting can be enabled to configure the VM quotas for users. You can define the number of VMs per user and limit the number of virtual machines using SSD, as shown in Figure 1-9. This helps restrict the costs associated with creating VMs for development and testing. Similar quotas can be set on a per lab basis as well.

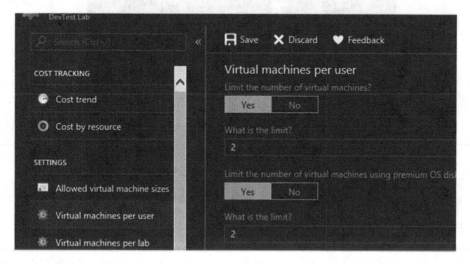

Figure 1-9. *Virtual machines per user*

- **Lab settings**. Here you can change users' default permission from reader access to contributor access, as shown in Figure 1-10.

Figure 1-10. *Lab settings*

- **Auto-shutdown** and **Auto-start**. These settings are found under DevTest Labs ➤ Schedules. While running a lab environment, they help reduce the charges incurred if the VMs can be automatically shut down after use, as shown in Figure 1-11.

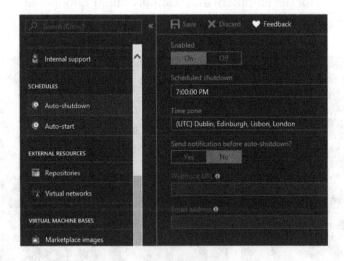

Figure 1-11. *Auto-shutdown configuration*

Auto-start settings are available to start VMs at a specific time as shown in Figure 1-12. This reduces the administrative overhead of manually starting the machines every day after shutdown.

Figure 1-12. *Auto-start configuration*

- **Repositories**. These are found under Configuration and policies ➤ External resources ➤ Repositories. You can link your artifact repository here. GitHub and VSTS repositories can be linked to the DevTest Lab, as shown in Figure 1-13. The parameters given show how the GitHub repository is linked. Provide the Git clone URI, personal access token, and the Artifacts folder path.

Figure 1-13. *Repositories in DevTest Labs*

- **Custom images**. These are added to DevTest Labs by selecting Configuration and policies ➤ Virtual machine bases ➤ Custom images. A custom virtual hard disk (VHD) can be uploaded to Azure Storage using PowerShell, and you can use this VHD to create a custom image.

Storage in IaaS

Azure virtual machines use Azure Storage page blobs in the back end to store virtual machine hard disks. There are two categories of storage for VMs: standard and premium. Standard storage provides magnetic HDD-based disks; whereas premium storage supports high-speed SSD-based disks.

The storage used for placing the VM disks can be managed by the user or the Azure platform. When the underlying storage is managed by the user, it is called an *unmanaged disk*. When it is managed by the platform, it is called a *managed disk*. In this section, we explore the different aspects of VM storage in IaaS.

Unmanaged Disks

When the user is in charge of the underlying storage used by VM disks, the user must consider the maximum number of VMs using storage, disk I/O requirements, the number of VHDs, and so forth; for example, a single storage account can handle only 20,000 read/write requests per second. The maximum throughput for a single blob is up to 60 MiB per second or 500 requests per second. These limitations are relevant to large environments with hundreds of VMs. When using unmanaged disks, VMs should be distributed across multiple storage accounts to avoid resource contention. These details should be etched out during the design phase.

Unmanaged disks are best used in small-scale environments where cost is a major deciding factor. Unmanaged disks are charged only for the data actually stored in them, and not for the entire provisioned size. If you have a provisioned 100 GB disk and stored only 20 GB of data on it, for example, you are charged only for 20 GB of storage.

Managed Disks

Managed disks were introduced in 2017 to reduce the VM storage management overhead, because details like the placement of disks are handled by the Azure platform. Managed disks add an additional layer of availability at the storage level for VMs already placed in an availability set. VM disks are placed in different storage stamps to avoid a single point of failure from a storage perspective. With unmanaged disks, the user must ensure that the VM disks in availability sets are placed in different storage accounts, thereby adding complexity to the design. With managed disks, you can handle disks as independent resources and apply RBAC permissions.

Managed disks are available in fixed sizes, in both standard hard disk drive (HDD) and premium SSD format. The following disks sizes are available as of writing this book: 32 GB, 64 GB, 128 GB, 256 GB, 512 GB, 1 TB, 2 TB, and 4 TB. The pricing model is different from that of unmanaged disks, because storage charges are for the entire provisioned size. The pricing model should be factored when planning for large-scale deployments, because the total cost is higher when compared to unmanaged disks. In addition to storage costs, the number of storage transactions and outbound data transfers are chargeable for both managed and unmanaged disks.

Standard and Premium Storage

Standard storage offers general-purpose storage based on HDD for blobs, tables, queues, and files. Page blob storage is used for holding persistent VM disks. Standard storage is limited in terms of disk performance because it can provide only a maximum of 500 IOPS and up to 60 MB per second of bandwidth per disk. Azure Storage has built-in redundancy, where three copies of the data are stored in a datacenter at any given time. This redundancy level is called *locally redundant storage* (LRS). Additional redundancy levels are available as geo-redundant storage (GRS), zone-redundant storage (ZRS), and read-access geo-redundant storage (RA-GRS). (These are discussed in detail in Chapter 4). Standard storage supports all redundancy types except ZRS in unmanaged disks, and only LRS in managed disks.

Premium storage offers higher performance for applications hosted in Azure, because they use solid-state drives in the back end. These are fixed-size disks ranging from 32 GB to 4 TB. The premium disk types are P4, P6, P10, P20, P30, P40, and P50. While standard storage IOPs are limited to 500 per disk, premium storage offers higher IOPs, depending on the disk variant. P20 offers 2300 IOPS. P30 offers 5000 IOPS. P40 and P50 offer the highest IOPS available (i.e., 7500 IOPS/disk). They also offer the highest throughput (i.e., 250 MB/second).

Both managed disks and unmanaged disks have premium storage versions available. With premium managed disks, the disk is placed in premium storage in the back end, where it provides the resiliency associated with managed disks and the performance benefit of premium storage. The storage cost is linked to the total provisioned size of the disk. The redundancy type for premium storage is limited to LRS.

VM Disks

Each VM is created with an OS disk and a temporary disk. They are stored as VHD files in standard or premium storage. The VMs are stored as gen1 Hyper-V machines in the back end, so the VHDX format is not supported.

- **OS disk**. By default, the OS disk size is 127 GB for Windows images and 30 GB for Linux images. Size can be expanded up to 2 TB, even though page blobs support up to 4 TB, which is the maximum size possible for data disks; however, OS disks currently support only up to 2 TB.

- **Temporary disk**. The size of the temporary disk depends on the VM SKU. The temporary disk is used for storing any temporary application logs, page files, or swap files. The temporary disk is listed as the D drive in the provisioned VM. Any data stored in this disk

will be lost in the event of a VM reboot/redeployment
or maintenance activity. In the back end, this disk
is provisioned from the Hyper-V host, and data loss
is possible if the VM is moved to a new host during
reboot/redeployment and a new temporary disk is
allocated from the current host.

- **Data disk**. You can attach additional data disks to
  your virtual machine, depending on your storage
  requirements. Ideally, all application data should
  be stored in data disks. The number of data disks
  that can be attached depends on the VM SKU; it is a
  design consideration when selecting SKUs. There are
  a maximum of 64 data disks and the maximum disk
  capacity of a VM is 256 TB. The VM SKUs that support
  64 data disks are the F series, L series, M series, and G
  series. Even though the maximum size of a single data
  disk is 4 TB, you can create drives with sizes greater
  that 4 TB by combining the data disks together using
  storage spaces.

To add a data disk to a VM from the Azure portal, select **Virtual
machine ➤ Settings ➤ Disks**, and click the **Add data disk** button, as
shown in Figure 1-14. You can choose to either create a disk or attach an
existing data disk.

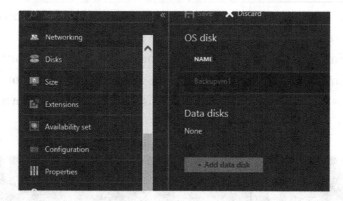

Figure 1-14. *Add data disk*

During VM creation, there is a wizard to attach an unmanaged disk, as shown in Figure 1-15. Specify the size of the disk, the type of storage, and the storage container where the VHD should be stored to create the disk.

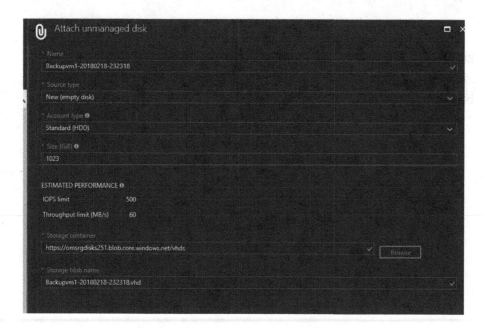

Figure 1-15. *Attach unmanaged disk*

Here we have selected to create and attach an empty disk. However, you can also attach an existing data disk in blob storage.

With managed disks, when you click the **Add data disk** button during VM creation, you have the option to create a new managed disk or select from an existing managed disk not being used by any VM, as shown in Figure 1-16.

Figure 1-16. *Create or attach managed disk*

In the **Create managed disk** wizard, provide the disk name, resource group, account type, source type, and the size of the disk, as shown in Figure 1-17. The source type can be an empty disk or an existing disk from blob storage or a snapshot of a disk.

Figure 1-17. *Create a managed disk*

Figure 1-18 shows a simple VM disk layout with an OS disk, temp disk, and data disk.

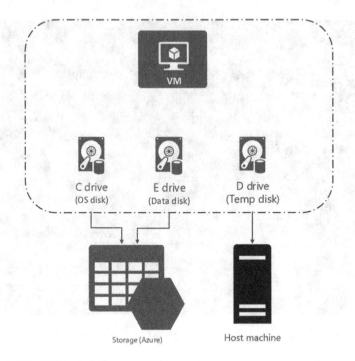

Figure 1-18. *VM disk layout*

General-Purpose v2 Storage

Azure Storage is classified as general-purpose v1, general-purpose v2, and blob. Of this, general-purpose storage accounts support all types, including blobs, files, queues, and tables; whereas blob storage supports only block blobs. Earlier, the hot and cold tiers of storage were supported only in blob storage. General-purpose v2 storage was announced in December 2017. It supports all the features of Azure Storage, along with hot, cold, and archival tiers for blob storage. The archival tier offers low-cost storage options for long-term retention of infrequently accessed data, and it should be incorporated in the architecture for similar use cases.

Azure Networking

Azure provides isolated virtual networks (VNet) for interconnecting devices and providing secure communication. In addition to providing connectivity between resources in a given VNet, Azure networking provides Internet connectivity to on-prem resources using hybrid connectivity options. Basic firewall and traffic monitoring capabilities are built into the networking layer.

Default Segmentation Using VNet

Azure VNets are logically isolated from each other unless they are explicitly connected via options like VPN or VNet peering. Each VNet has its own address space, which can be subdivided into multiple subnets. Default routing exists between the subnets in a VNet. Traffic is allowed to flow between them unless blocked by network security groups or custom rules. You can create a new VNet from the Azure portal by selecting **Create a resource ➤ Network ➤ Virtual network**, as shown in Figure 1-19.

Figure 1-19. *Create virtual network*

During a VNet creation, the address space and subnets should be defined. Any VMs connecting to the virtual network and subnet get addresses leased by a Dynamic Host Configuration Protocol (DHCP) service running in the back end based on the defined network range. If required, additional address spaces and subnets can be added later from the VNet settings.

Azure service endpoints are a relatively new feature that allows you to connect to Azure services via the internal VNet endpoints for secure communication. Currently, it is available for Azure Storage, SQL Database, and SQL Data Warehouse (preview). This is covered in detail in Chapter 7.

Once created, you can select the VNet when you create a VM in the same region. The list of all connected devices can be seen by selecting **Virtual network ➤ Settings ➤ Connected devices**, as shown in Figure 1-20.

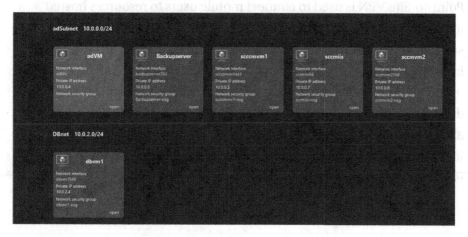

Figure 1-20. *Connected devices*

Azure VNet also provides a diagrammatic representation of all of your connected resources, which can be seen at VNet ➤ Monitoring ➤ Diagram, as shown in Figure 1-21. Here you can see which VMs are connected to subnets inside the network.

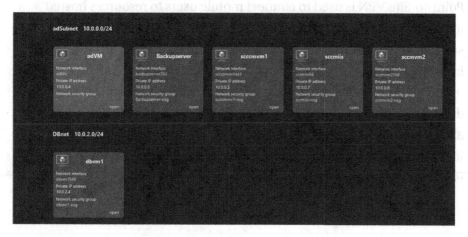

Figure 1-21. *Virtual network diagram*

Configure Hybrid Connectivity

There are three ways to connect an on-prem environment to Azure: Point-to-Site, Site-to-Site, and ExpressRoute. An Azure VPN gateway subnet and an Azure VPN gateway are the prerequisites for creating a hybrid connection from an Azure VNet. A gateways subnet is where the Azure virtual network gateways connect.

There are two types of VPN gateways available in Azure: policy based and route based. The type of gateway depends on the protocols supported in your on-premise devices. The policy-based VPN gateway in Azure supports IKEv1; whereas the route-based gateway supports IKEv2. The route-based gateway is the recommended option since it supports advanced configurations such as multisite connections, point-to-site VPNs, and site-to-site VPN coexistence, and so forth.

Point-to-Site VPN

Point-to-Site VPN is used to connect mobile users to resources hosted in Azure VNet over an encrypted VPN tunnel. This type of connection is suitable for mobile users who want to access Azure resources securely from a public network. The connection is secured using SSTP or IKEv2 protocols. Authentication is done using Azure certificates or Azure AD domain controller integration with a RADIUS server. The IKEv2 VPN allows Mac devices to connect to the VPN. It does not need a public IP, and it can use the Internet connection available for the user device. Figure 1-22 is a high-level overview of how a Point-to-Site VPN works.

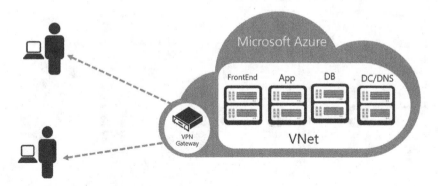

Figure 1-22. *Point-to-site VPN*

Site-to-Site VPN

If you want to extend your on-premise datacenter to Azure via VPN, then Site-to-Site VPN should be configured. It needs an on-premise supported VPN device and an available public IP. The VPN connection is established between the VPN device and the Azure Virtual Network gateway associated with the virtual network. The protocol used for the connection is IPsec/IKE (IKEv1 or IKEv2). You can also connect multiple on-premise networks to a VNet in Azure to cater to a head office/branch office scenario. Once the Site-to-Site VPN is configured, you can connect to VMs in Azure using their internal private IPs from on-premise devices.

Figure 1-23 is a sample architecture for an Azure hybrid network using Site-to-Site VPN.

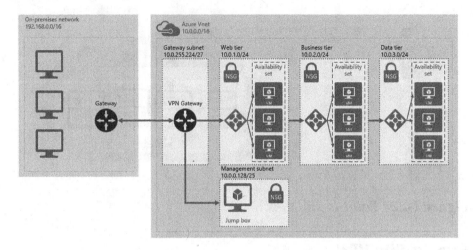

Figure 1-23. *Site-to-Site VPN sample architecture*

ExpressRoute

ExpressRoute is a private connection between resources in Azure and on-premise datacenter networks. In this case, network traffic does not traverse the Internet, and hence, ExpressRoute connections are faster, more reliable, and more secure than any other hybrid connection options. It is the only hybrid connection option backed by an uptime SLA. There are three connectivity models: a cloud exchange provider's Ethernet exchange, a point-to-point Ethernet connection, and Microsoft cloud connected as part of a WAN MPLS cloud.

Figure 1-24 shows a sample architecture for an Azure hybrid network using ExpressRoute.

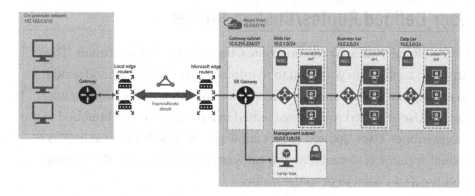

Figure 1-24. ExpressRoute sample architecture

Routing in VNets

When an Azure VNet is created, default system routes are added to the VNet route table. There are three types of possible routes in a VNet: system routes, user-defined routes, and BGP routes (ExpressRoute).

System Routes

System routes take care of the following network traffic:

- Communication between VMs connected to the same subnet

- Traffic flow from one subnet to another inside a VNet

- Internet traffic originating from the VMs

- Traffic to another VNet via VPN gateway

- Traffic to an on-premise network via a VPN gateway

User-Defined Routes/Custom Routes

User-defined routes, or custom routes, override the default routes. They are often used when you want to manipulate the traffic flow and send it to an external device, such as a firewall or any other traffic monitoring device. User-defined routes are created in a route table and attached to the target subnet. User-defined routes allow you to specify the next hop as a virtual appliance, virtual network gateway, virtual network, the Internet, or nothing if you want to drop the traffic.

BGP Route (ExpressRoute)

When a hybrid connection exists with an on-premise gateway that uses BGP and Azure VNet via ExpressRoute or VPN, routes are exchanged via BGP protocol. In a scenario where BGP routes and user-defined routes exist with the default routes, and multiple routes have the same prefix, the route is selected in the following order of priority:

1. user-defined route

2. BGP route

3. system route

Summary

This chapter introduced you to the major components of Azure IaaS under the three main pillars: compute, storage, and network. These building blocks play a major role in all infrastructure architecture decisions, and they should be carefully chosen to fit into diverse use cases and scenarios.

CHAPTER 2

Compute Migration

While planning to migrate from on-prem environments to Azure, the similarities and dissimilarities of the design concepts should be taken into consideration. In the initial phases, instead of complete migration, organizations typically prefer to use a hybrid cloud approach where part of the resources remain on-premise, and the architecture is designed to leverage Azure resources as well. Whatever the preferred approach is, it is important for an architect to understand the existing infrastructure landscape and to identify equivalent components in Azure to facilitate a smooth migration.

This chapter maps the on-premise architecture components to counterparts in Azure. It explores the options available to execute migration tasks, and it overviews the steps involved in an actual migration.

Migrating Compute Workloads to Azure

Migrating workloads to Azure is done at different phases, which are logically summarized in the following order (see Figure 2-1).

© Shijimol Ambi Karthikeyan 2018
S. Ambi Karthikeyan, *Practical Microsoft Azure IaaS*,
https://doi.org/10.1007/978-1-4842-3763-2_2

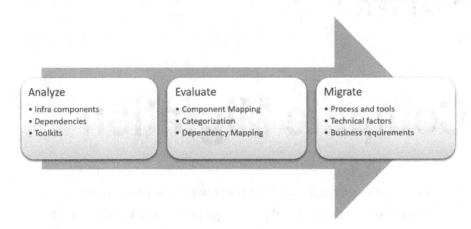

Figure 2-1. *Migration workflow*

Analyze

A comprehensive document and an architecture diagram should be available to clearly understand the existing infrastructure layout. The interdependencies of the components should be etched out for clarity. For environments where this interrelationship is not documented—for example, legacy environments, consider using options like the Microsoft Assessment and Planning (MAP) toolkit to generate a comprehensive report of existing environment.

Evaluate

You should have a list of the infrastructure components (and their dependencies) that need to be migrated. These components should be evaluated and mapped against the equivalent services in Azure. You might have to further subdivide your components into basic services; for example, when migrating a server to Azure, you consume compute, storage, and network services. A mapping of the compute power to the available instance types in Azure should be done along with the mapping of storage.

You may also need to make a decision on the kind of storage to be used, which is a decision between premium vs. standard storage and managed vs. unmanaged disks.

Migrate

After the assessment and evaluation phase, the primary decision involves the migration process and tools. This depends on technical factors such as infrastructure type (i.e., virtualized or not, type of virtualization used, OS versions, and etc.). The business dependencies—such as consumption models, SLAs, acceptable downtimes, and so forth—should also be factored when selecting the migration method.

Physical Servers

Even though the majority of workloads in modern-day datacenters use some form of virtualization, some physical servers are still being used for special or specific use cases. For example, if you are running applications that need dedicated compute capacity without any processor sharing, then physical servers are still the preferred option. Legacy applications are another complicated possibility; they may still run from the original physical servers due to ambiguity around design and dependencies. In both cases, careful planning is required in the migration plan.

The end goal is to convert the source machine to a compatible format in Microsoft Azure. One important factor is that in back-end Azure IaaS VMs are basically Gen 1 Hyper-V VMs. The virtual hard disk is stored in Azure Storage as a page blob in VHD format. this chapter focuses purely on migration rather than setting up a fresh environment using Azure IaaS followed by migration of applications, although that could be the best bet in certain scenarios.

Use Microsoft documentation to check compatibility when migrating legacy applications and operating systems. A common scenario for legacy applications is the migration of Windows Server 2003 to Azure. Customers can upload the VHD of a machine running Windows Server 2003 to Azure even though it is past end of support; however, the customer needs to have a customer support agreement. The document at `https://support.microsoft.com/en-us/help/2721672/microsoft-server-software-support-for-microsoft-azure-virtual-machines` provides information on all the supported Microsoft application and server versions in Azure.

Physical servers might have special hardware requirements, such as PRI cards or graphical processing units (GPUs). During the evaluation phase, the availability of equivalent components in Azure should be confirmed; for example, applications running on physical servers with GPUs can be migrated to Azure N series virtual machines with NVIDIA GPUs.

Migration Option 1: Upload VHD

Converting physical server to virtual hard disk (VHD) format and then creating virtual machines using those VHDs is one method of migration to Azure. You can convert the physical server to VHD format using tools such as Sysinternal Disk2VHD or System Center Virtual Machine Manager. The VHD can be sysprepped and uploaded to Microsoft storage by using PowerShell, AzCopy, or Azure Storage blob APIs. This VHD can be eventually used to create the VM in Azure. See `https://docs.microsoft.com/en-us/azure/virtual-machines/windows/upload-generalized-managed` for more information.

Migration Option 2: Azure Site Recovery (ASR)

Azure Site Recovery (ASR) is a disaster recovery solution for physical servers. The physical server–based environment can be replicated to Azure using ASR. The same approach can be used for migration, where the replicated environment is failed over and then continues to run from Azure. An additional VM or physical machine should be available on-premise to set up the ASR components (i.e., the configuration server and the process server). These components have the following two major roles:

- **Configuration server**. Manages data replication and coordinated communication to Azure.

- **Process server**. The data being sent to Azure is cached, compressed, and encrypted by the process server component. A *mobility agent* is deployed to all target machines to be replicated.

Another component, called the *master target server*, comes bundled with this. Its function is to manage replication during failback, which is not relevant in a migration scenario. The process of the physical server to Azure migration is explained next.

Prerequisites for Physical Server to Azure Migration

The following steps should be completed in the initial phase.

1. Set up the Recovery Services vault in the Azure portal.

2. Install and configure the configuration server on-premise using the unified setup. From the Recovery Services vault, select **Get started ➤ Site Recovery ➤ Prepare infrastructure ➤ Protection goal** (see Figure 2-2).

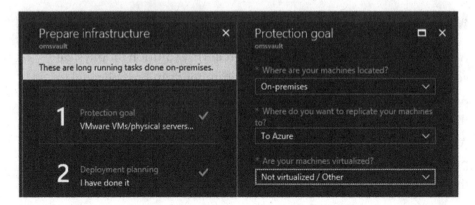

Figure 2-2. *Select protection goal*

3. Confirm that deployment planning is completed. You can download and execute the deployment planner to get information on VM eligibility, possible RPOs with the allocated bandwidth, Azure and on-premise infrastructure requirements, VM grouping recommendations, and estimated charges. For VMware environments, you can also use the new Azure Migrate feature, which is explained in the next section.

4. To progress to the next step, select the **Yes, I have done it** option (see Figure 2-3).

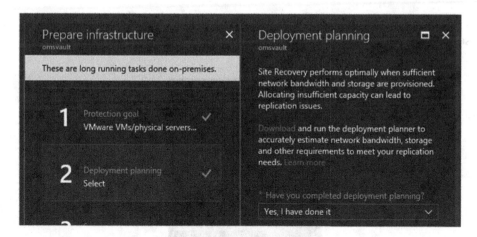

Figure 2-3. *Deployment planning*

5. Click **+Configuration Server** (see Figure 2-4).

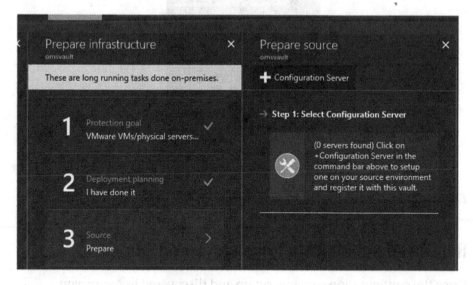

Figure 2-4. *Add configuration Server*

You are taken to a set of instructions on how to install the configuration server (see Figure 2-5).

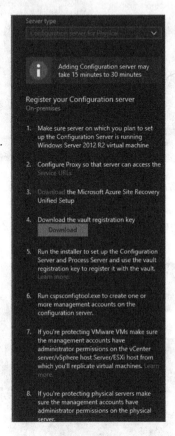

Figure 2-5. *Install configuration server*

Replicate and Migrate Physical Servers to Azure

Once the configuration server is set up and discovered in Azure, you need to complete the next steps in prepare infrastructure phase. Complete the target environment configuration, where you define the target environment in Azure (i.e., the resource group) and ensure that a compatible storage, network, and so forth, are available in the subscription. Next, you need to configure a replication policy that refines the replication intervals, RPOs, and so forth.

Now let's look at what needs to be done at the physical server end to enable the replication.

1. Set up the registry key entry (see Figure 2-6).

Figure 2-6. *Set registry key*

2. Enable the following through a firewall in **Allowed apps and features** (see Figure 2-7).

   - File and Printer Sharing

   - Windows Management Instrumentation

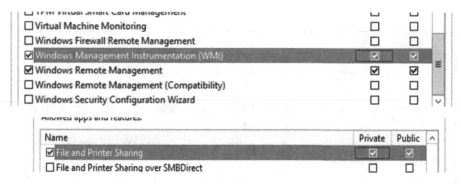

Figure 2-7. *Allow apps and features*

47

3. Add an account that has admin privileges in the target physical machine in the cspsconfigtool, which is in the location on the configuration server shown in Figure 2-8.

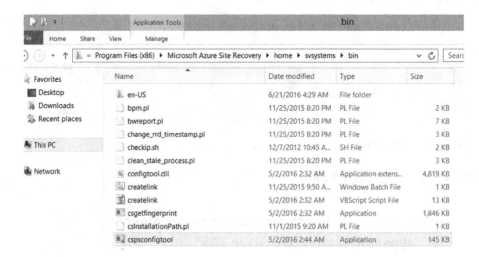

Figure 2-8. *cspsconfigtool location*

4. Click the Add Account button (see Figure 2-9).

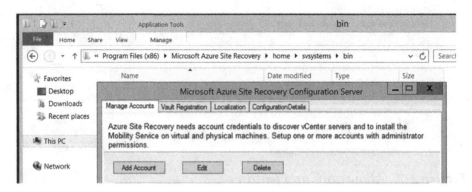

Figure 2-9. *Add account*

5. In this case, the physical machine was not added to the domain; hence, a local admin user was added. The friendly name can be anything; it is just to identify that account in Azure portal (see Figure 2-10).

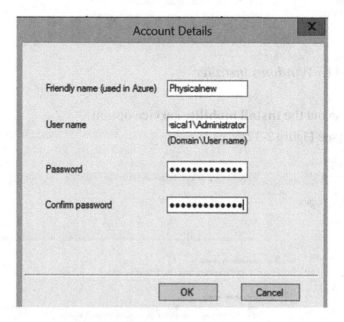

Figure 2-10. *Account information*

6. Now you can install the mobility agent on the physical server. The installer is in the configuration server at the location shown in Figure 2-11. You need to select the installer based on the operating system type. In this case, the Windows installer was selected.

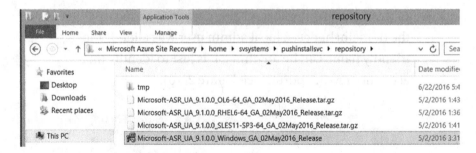

Figure 2-11. *Windows Installer*

7. Select the **Install mobility service** option
    (see Figure 2-12).

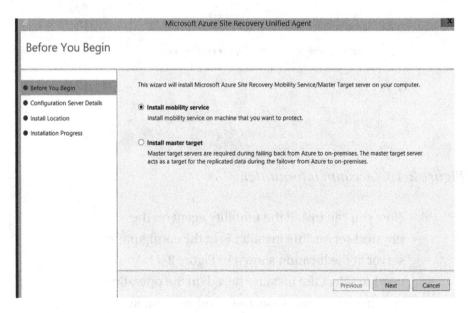

Figure 2-12. *Install mobility service*

8. Enter the configuration server IP and passphrase (see Figure 2-13).

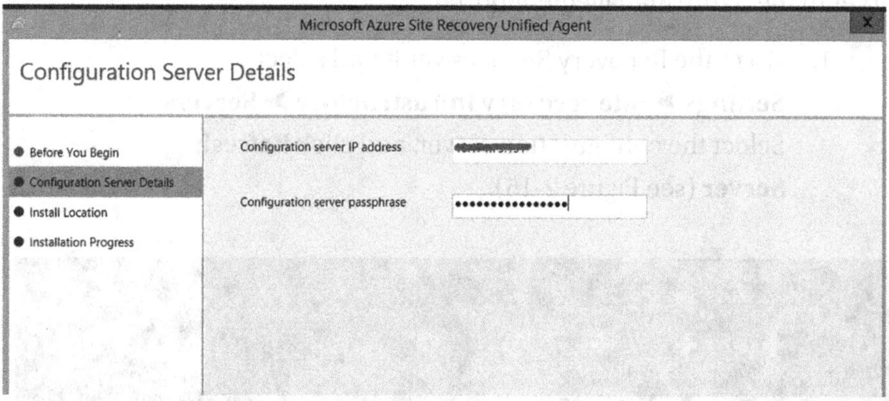

Figure 2-13. IP and passphrase

9. Specify the install location.

This is all that is required. You can go to the next step and wait for the installation to be complete (see Figure 2-14).

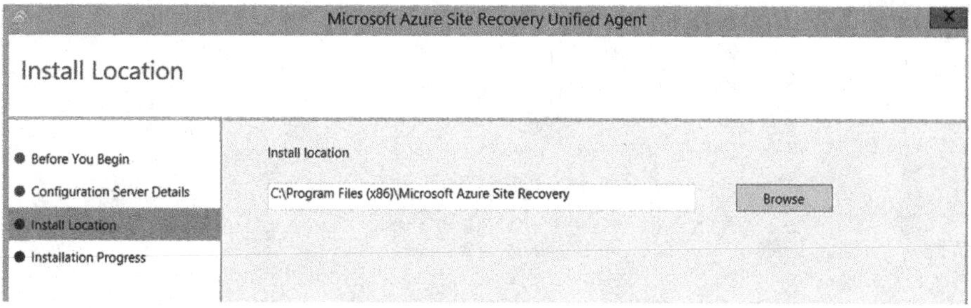

Figure 2-14. Install location

Azure Portal Steps

Now that the mobility agent is installed, you can refresh the configuration server in the Azure management portal.

1. Go to the Recovery Services vault and select
   Settings ➤ Site recovery infrastructure ➤ Servers.
   Select the configuration server, and click **Refresh
   Server** (see Figure 2-15).

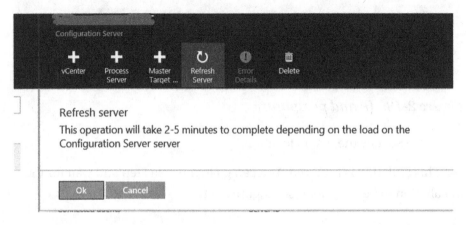

Figure 2-15. Refresh server

2. Click OK. Once the refresh is completed, the new
    physical server is reflected in the connected agents
    list (see Figure 2-16).

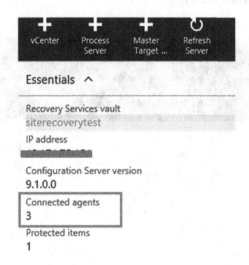

Figure 2-16. *Connected agents*

3. Enable replication for your physical server. In the
    Management portal, go to the Recovery Services
    vault and select **Settings** ➤ **Site Recovery** ➤ **Enable
    replication** (see Figure 2-17).

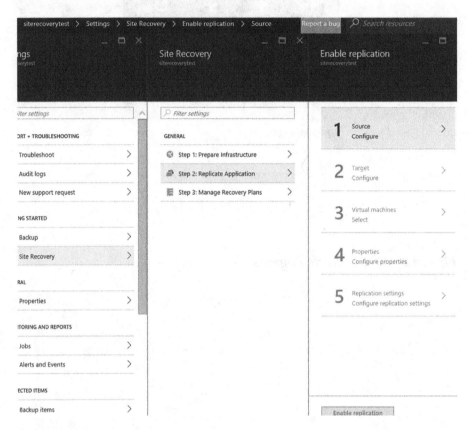

Figure 2-17. *Enable replication*

4. Enter the source. This is your configuration server. The machine type is the physical machine. The process server in this installation is the same as the configuration server (see Figure 2-18).

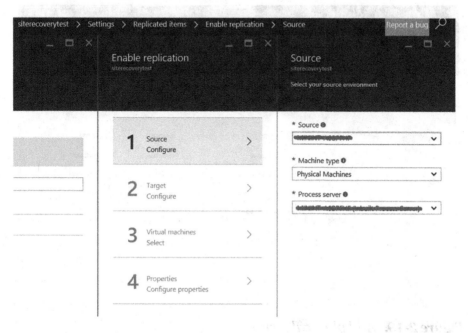

Figure 2-18. *Select source*

5. Configure the target environment in Azure. Select
    the target physical server. Click **+Physical machine**
    (see Figure 2-19).

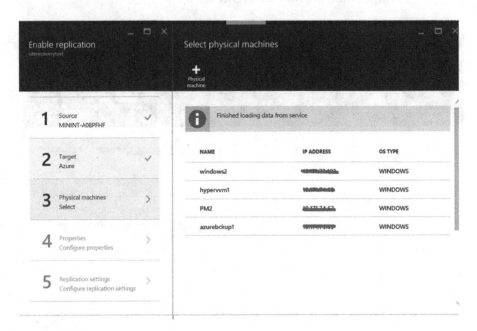

Figure 2-19. *Add physical server*

6. Enter the information about your on-prem physical
    server: server name, IP address, and the OS type
    (see Figure 2-20).

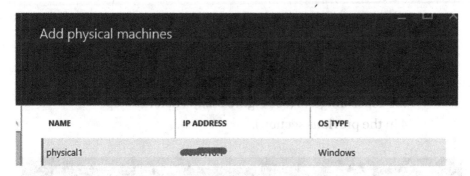

Figure 2-20. *Machine details*

7. Click OK. Once the server is added, it is listed in the
    blade. Select the server and click OK (see Figure 2-21).

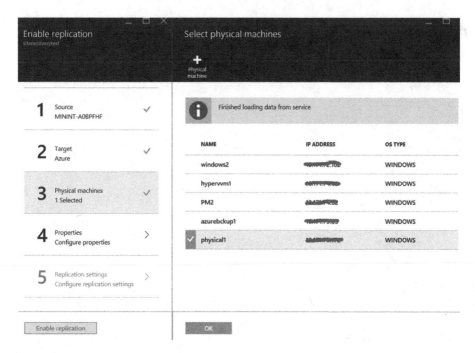

Figure 2-21. *Select physical server*

8. If the agent is detected by the portal, you are able to
    select the disks that you want to back up (i.e., disks
    other than the OS disks). From the account drop-
    down menu, select the account that you created in
    the cspsconfigtool (see Figure 2-22). (Refer to step
    4 in the previous section).

Figure 2-22. *Select account*

9. On the **Configure replication settings** page, select
   the replication policy that you created earlier (see
   Figure 2-23).

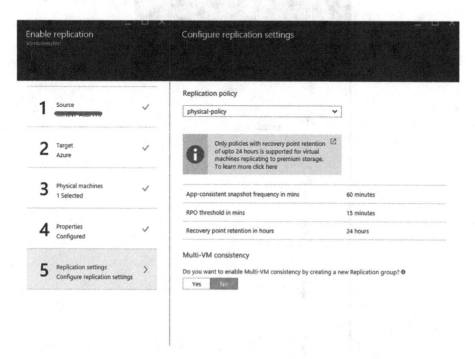

Figure 2-23. *Select replication policy*

10.   All the steps are done. Click **Enable replication** to protect your on-prem physical server (see Figure 2-24).

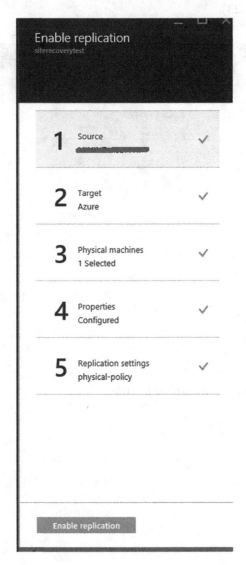

Figure 2-24.   *Enable replication*

Once the machines are replicated and available in Azure, they are listed as healthy and protected. To enable the migration, you need to do a planned failover to Azure. Select the target machine in the Recovery Services vault and then select **Protected items**. This takes you to a screen with all types of failovers listed. For a clean migration, select planned failover from the available options (see Figure 2-25).

Figure 2-25. *Planned replication*

To complete the migration, confirm the failover direction in the next step, which is from on-premise to Azure. The virtual machine is up and running in the Azure portal after the migration.

VMware Virtualization

Environments virtualized using VMware can also make use of the ASR as a migration tool. This process needs a configuration server to be set up in the on-premise VMware site to coordinate the replication.

The Configuration Server

The configuration server can be downloaded in OVF format from the Azure portal and set using the instructions shown in Figure 2-26.

Figure 2-26. *Add configuration server*

During the open virtualization format (OVF) configuration, you need to provide the vCenter server or vSphere ESXi server to connect to the server. After connecting the vCenter or ESXi, the associated VMs are reflected in the Azure portal for replication. The subsequent steps for enabling the replication and then migrating these machines are the same as that of physical servers.

Azure Migrate

Azure Migrate is a tool that helps with migration planning to Azure. At the time of writing this book, Azure Migrate supported VMware environments managed by vCenter servers 5.5, 6.0, and 6.5.

Azure Migrate performs an assessment of VMware-hosted machines and provides information on whether there are any constraints on migrating the on-premise VMs. The assessment is done using a virtual appliance called Azure Migrate Collector, which can be downloaded from the Azure portal. You need to create an Azure Migrate project in the Azure portal.

1. Search "azure migrate" in the Azure portal **All services** and select **Migration projects** (see Figure 2-27).

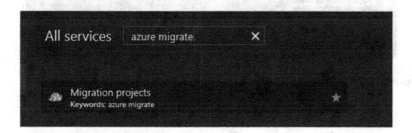

Figure 2-27. *Select migration projects*

2. Add a migration project by providing the basic information: project name, subscription, resource group name, and location. The migration project holds the metadata on on-premise workloads. Click **Discover machines** in Azure Migrate to get step-by-step instructions on the discovery and assessment process. The open virtual appliance (OVA) to set up the collector appliance can be downloaded from this page (see Figure 2-28).

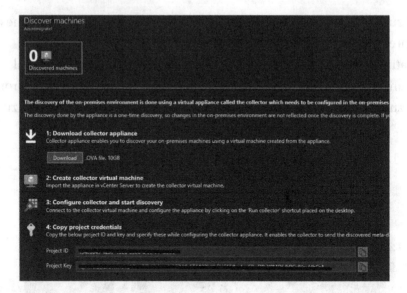

Figure 2-28. *Discover machines*

3. After setting up the collector appliance, click
Run collector in the collector virtual machine to
open the Collector wizard. Confirm that all the
prerequisites are met (see Figure 2-29).

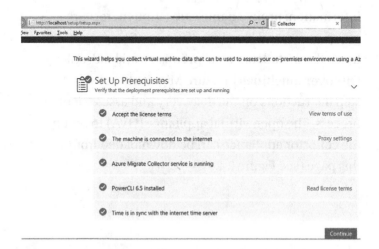

Figure 2-29. *Check prerequisites*

4. Connect to the vCenter instance. You can use a read-only account to get the information (see Figure 2-30).

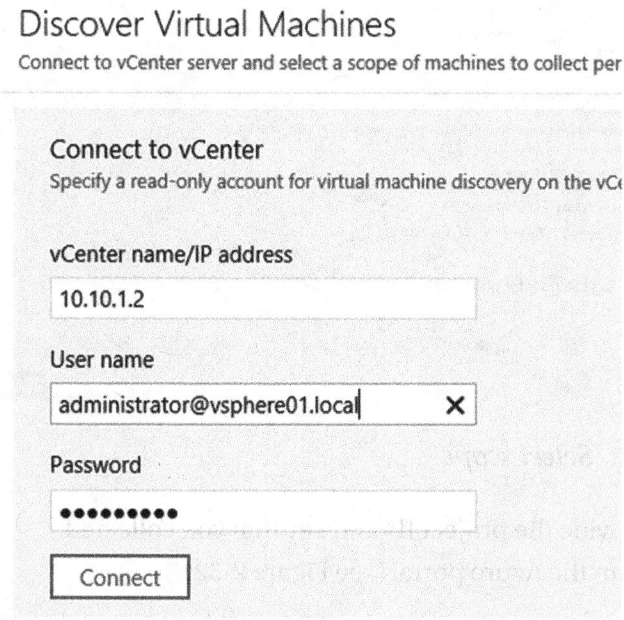

Discover Virtual Machines

Connect to vCenter server and select a scope of machines to collect per

Connect to vCenter

Specify a read-only account for virtual machine discovery on the vC

vCenter name/IP address

```
10.10.1.2
```

User name

```
administrator@vsphere01.local        ✕
```

Password

```
••••••••••
```

Connect

Figure 2-30. *Discover vCenter/ ESXi*

5.   After connecting the vCenter, select the scope
     of inventory, and click the Continue button (see
     Figure 2-31).

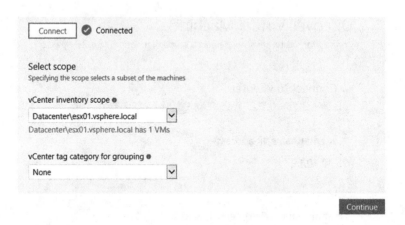

Figure 2-31.   *Select scope*

6.   Provide the project ID and key that you collected
     from the Azure portal (see Figure 2-32).

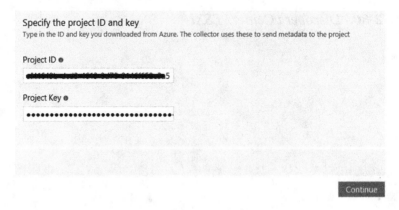

Figure 2-32.   *Project ID and Key*

The data collection process starts and the information is shown in the Azure portal (see Figure 2-33).

Essentials

Machines	Assessments	Groups	Learn more
9	107	102	Overview of Azure ☐ Migrate

Figure 2-33. Data collection output

You can create an assessment of the VMs that you plan to migrate. This is useful in scenarios in which there is dependency between the VMs.

1. Click **Create assessment** in the Azure migrate project. Create a new group and add the required VMs after the assessment is completed (see Figure 2-34).

Select or create a group
○ Create New   ○ Use Existing

fibgroup1   ✓

Add machines to the group
Select all   Clear selection

	NAME
☑	DataTierVM01
	MiddleTierVM01
☑	WEB
☐	MiddleTierVM02

Figure 2-34. Create assessment

2. Review the information about the migration
    readiness and the monthly cost estimates
    (see Figure 2-35).

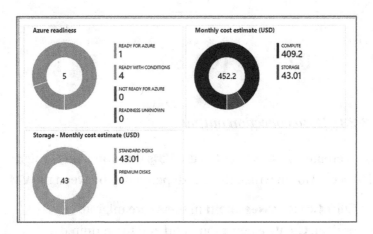

Figure 2-35. *Readiness and monthly estimates*

3. If you further drill down into Azure readiness
    information, you see the VM instance mapping and
    any incompatibilities (see Figure 2-36).

NAME	AZURE VM READINESS	AZURE VM SIZE	SUGGESTED TOOL
DataTierVM01	⚠ Conditionally supported Windows Server OS	Standard_A4_v2	🖧 Azure Site Recovery
MiddleTierVM01	⚠ Conditionally supported Windows Server OS	Standard_A0	🖧 Azure Site Recovery
WEB	✅	Standard_A0	🖧 Azure Site Recovery

Figure 2-36. *VM compatibility*

The information made available by Azure Migrate acts as input
to the actual migration process using ASR; for example, it flags any
incompatibilities and the right VM size to select when you do the failover.

Hyper-V Virtualization

VHDs from Hyper-V environments are uploaded to Azure Storage and converted to images to create VMs. Alternatively, you can use ASR to replicate and failover the VMs to Azure. Gen 2 VMs are not currently supported in Azure, and hence Gen 2 Hyper-V machines VHDX files should be converted to VHD before uploading to Azure Storage. When using ASR, the VHDX files are automatically converted to VHD.

Migration Using ASR

ASR provides a more reliable and easier method of migration with minimal administrative overhead. Independent Hyper-V hosts and hosts managed by SCVMM are supported for migration. The basic process remains the same: you add the Hyper-V Host/SCVMM to ASR and then replicate the VMs to Azure. We will look at how this is done for VMs in independent Hyper-V hosts because this seems to be the most common scenario.

1. Prepare the infrastructure in ASR. From the Recovery Services vault, go to **Get started** ➤ **Site Recovery** ➤ **Protection goal**, and select the Hyper-V to Azure option (see Figure 2-37).

Figure 2-37. Deployment planning

2. Similar to VMware environments, the deployment planner tool is also used for Hyper-V–based environments. Confirm that the deployment planning is completed (see Figure 2-38).

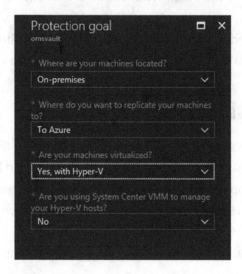

Figure 2-38. *Protection goal*

3. Add a Hyper-V site that is a logical group for your target Hyper-V host (see Figure 2-39).

Figure 2-39. *Add Hyper-V Site*

4. Add a Hyper-V server by installing the ASR Provider
    .exe. The vault credentials need to be downloaded to
    register the Hyper-V host with the Recovery Services
    vault. Follow the wizard instructions to complete the
    installation and configuration (see Figure 2-40).

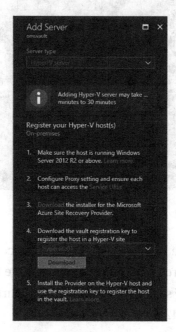

Figure 2-40. *Register Hyper-V host*

5. Once the installation and configuration of the ASR
    service provider is completed, the host is listed from
    the drop-down menu (see Figure 2-41).

Figure 2-41. *Add host*

6. Progress to the Replicate Application process.
    Select the source environment. The source location
    is the Hyper-V site that you had created earlier
    (see Figure 2-42).

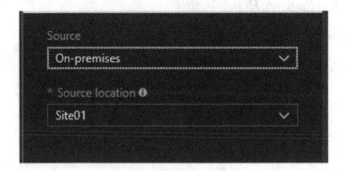

Figure 2-42. *Source environment*

7. Select the target Azure environment settings, such
    as the Azure Storage and Network (see Figure 2-43).
    ASR uses the selected storage and network during
    any failover activity.

Figure 2-43. *Storage and Network*

8. The VMs hosted in the Hyper-V hosted are listed in the Azure portal. Select the virtual machine to be replicated (see Figure 2-44).

Figure 2-44. Select VMs

9. Configure the VM properties (i.e., the OS type) and
    the disks to replicate to Azure (see Figure 2-45).

Figure 2-45. *Configure VM settings*

10. Select the replication policy, and click OK (see
    Figure 2-46).

Configure replication settings

Replication policy

SitePolicy01

Copy frequency	5 Minutes
Recovery point retention	2 Hours
App consistent snapshot frequency	1 Hour
Initial replication start time	Immediately
Encrypt data stored on Azure	Off
VMM settings	Not configured

Figure 2-46. *Select replication policy*

11.   Click **Enable Replication**. Once the replication
      is completed, the status of the VMs is listed in the
      Recovery Services vault under **Protected items ➤
      Replicated items** (see Figure 2-47).

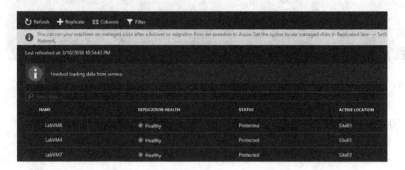

Figure 2-47.   View status

12.   Ensure that the replication health is listed as
      "healthy" and that the status is "protected". Click
      the VM that you want to migrate and click **Planned
      failover** to complete the migration.

Other Platforms

ASR is the primary Microsoft native tool for migrating workloads to Azure.
In addition to migrating physical and virtualized environments on-premise,
it can migrate workloads hosted in AWS to Azure. Even though its main
functionality is a *disaster recovery as a service* (DRaaS) solution, the
replication and planned migration options are handy in migration scenarios.
It also offers a test failover functionality for migration testing. Environments
can be created in Azure based on the replicated data, and then further tested
to ensure that the hosted applications are working fine before proceeding to
the actual migration. All of these functionalities are available on a pay-as-
you-go model, which makes the solution even more economical.

In addition to the native Microsoft solutions, third-party vendors provide tools that help with migrating the infrastructure to the cloud. Veeam offers a **Restore to Azure** option, which migrates VMware, Hyper-V, and physical workloads to Azure. Like ASR, it offers a test failover functionality to set up and test the environment before the failover.

Zerto is another vendor that offers migration services to many cloud service providers. If an organization has an existing investment in any of these vendor technologies, they can leverage the same for workload migration.

Summary

Meticulous planning and evaluation of the components are imperative when migrating on-premise hosted workloads to Azure. To ensure a hassle-free operation, it is particularly important that you select the right tool for the job. This chapter provided an overview of the migration considerations and tools available to move on-premise workloads hosted in physical, VMware, or Hyper-V environments to Azure.

CHAPTER 3

Storage and Network Migration

In the previous chapter, we went through the options available for migrating on-premise hosted workloads to Azure. While a holistic approach is important, it is also relevant to understand the different Azure network and storage options so as to map the services appropriately during a migration. This chapter focuses on storage and network considerations when migrating workloads to Azure.

Traditional Storage vs. Storage in Azure

The storage capabilities for on-premise workloads are provided either by local HDDs/SSDs in servers or storage solutions such as network attached storage (NAS) or storage area networks (SANs). In the Azure cloud landscape, the underlying storage is provided by *storage as a service* (SaaS) offerings, thereby removing the overhead of underlying storage management. However, we can draw parallels between different on-premise storage features and the options available in cloud.

© Shijimol Ambi Karthikeyan 2018
S. Ambi Karthikeyan, *Practical Microsoft Azure IaaS*,
https://doi.org/10.1007/978-1-4842-3763-2_3

RAID Configuration

Disks form the basic building blocks for on-premise storage. RAID (*redundant array of independent disks*) is used to distribute data across multiple disks for resiliency and improved performance. RAID is implemented as either hardware RAID or software RAID. Whereas hardware RAID uses a dedicated hardware controller and an associated processor, software RAID is done at the OS layer without any additional hardware requirements. There are several different RAID levels; the most common are RAID 0, RAID 1, RAID 5, RAID 6, and RAID 10.

- RAID 0 is used for stripping data across multiple disks, thereby resulting in improved performance. However, it does not provide resiliency, as the data is lost, even in single disk failures.

- RAID 1 is also called *disk mirroring*. All data blocks are written in two disks in parallel so that the data is available if even one of the disks fails. Once the failed disk is replaced, data is rebuilt from the available disk.

- RAID 5 stores data across multiple disks along with the parity bits. If one of the disks fails, data can be re-created from the remaining disks and parity. It offers a balance between speed and redundancy.

- RAID 6 strips the data across disks like RAID 5; however, it stores extra parity bits that help recover data even if two disks fail.

- RAID 10 combines the capabilities of RAID 1 and RAID 0, where data is stripped and mirrored across additional disks for optimal performance and resiliency.

Storage Replication in Azure

Azure has built-in replication for all storage accounts. Hence, there are three copies of the virtual hard disk in the same datacenter by default, offering resiliency similar to that of RAID 1. Even if one of the copies is unavailable, data is not lost and can be accessed from the other two copies. This default replication option is synchronous. It is called *locally redundant storage* (LRS). If the data is replicated to a different region asynchronously, there are six copies of data, and three of these copies are in a paired geographical region. All copies are mirror copies, like that in a RAID 1 configuration.

Storage Spaces Configuration

Azure Storage Spaces aggregates multiple data disks to create virtual disks inside Azure VMs at the OS level. We can draw parallels between this approach and a RAID 0 configuration, where data is spread across multiple disks. The only difference is that here the resiliency is taken care of by the underlying Azure storage layer. Storage Spaces offer a solution to the maximum disk size constraint in Azure. For example, the maximum size of data disks that can be attached to an Azure VM is 4 TB. If you want to have a drive size greater than 4 TB, you can do the same by adding multiple disks in a storage pool and then create a virtual disk from the pool.

Start by adding data disks to the Azure VM. This process is explained (with examples) in Chapter 1. After adding the data disks, the storage space configuration should be done from with the virtual machine's OS.

1. Open disk management and create a new storage pool with the disk management wizard (see Figure 3-1).

Figure 3-1. *Disk management wizard*

2.   Name the pool (see Figure 3-2).

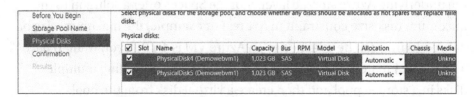

Figure 3-2. *Pool name*

3.   Select the disks to include in the storage pool
(see Figure 3-3).

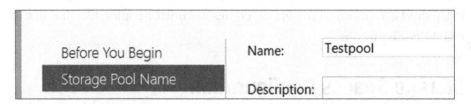

Figure 3-3. *Add disks*

4.   Review the properties and create the storage pool
(see Figure 3-4).

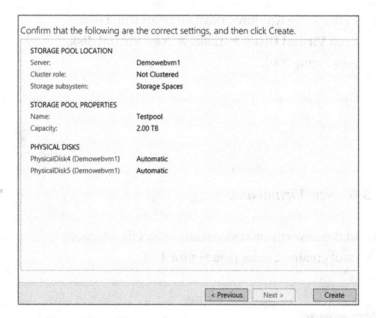

Figure 3-4. *Confirm settings*

Once created, the pool is listed in the server manager disk configuration window (see Figure 3-5).

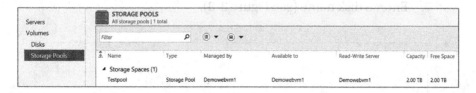

Figure 3-5. *Storage pools*

5. In the same windows, create a new virtual disk
    from **Virtual Disks ➤ Tasks ➤ New virtual disk**
    (see Figure 3-6).

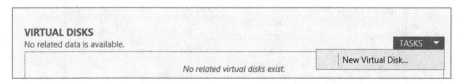

Figure 3-6. *New Virtual disk*

6. In the new virtual disk wizard, select the storage
    pool created earlier (see Figure 3-7).

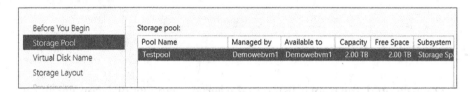

Figure 3-7. *Select storage pool*

7. Enter a disk name (see Figure 3-8).

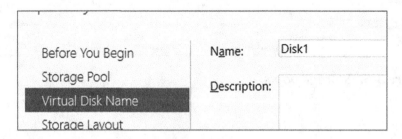

Figure 3-8. *Give the disk a name*

84

8. For storage layout, select a simple layout because resiliency is already provided by Azure storage (see Figure 3-9).

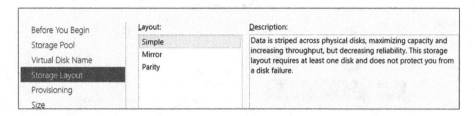

Figure 3-9. *Select resiliency type*

9. Select the provisioning type as either Thin or Fixed (see Figure 3-10).

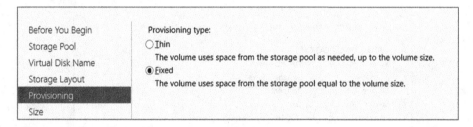

Figure 3-10. *Select provisioning type*

10. Specify the size of the virtual disk to be created from the available storage pool (see Figure 3-11).

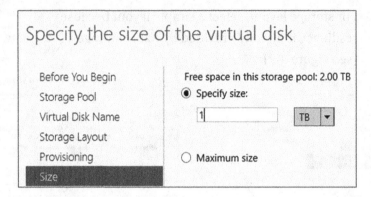

Figure 3-11. *Select disk size*

11. Confirm the settings and create the virtual disk (see Figure 3-12).

Confirm that the following are the correct settings, and then click Create.

VIRTUAL DISK LOCATION
Server: Demowebvm1
Subsystem: Storage Spaces
Storage pool name: Testpool
Status: OK
Free space: 2.00 TB

VIRTUAL DISK PROPERTIES
Name: Disk1
Storage tiers: Disabled
Storage layout: Simple
Provisioning type: Fixed
Requested size: 1.00 TB

Figure 3-12. *Confirm settings*

12. The virtual disk is listed in the server manager. Right-click the disk and select **New Volume** (see Figure 3-13).

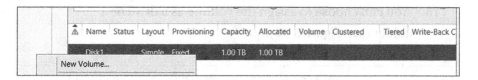

Figure 3-13. *Create a new volume*

13. In the new volume wizard, select the virtual disk (see Figure 3-14).

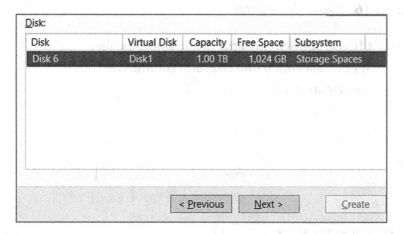

Figure 3-14. *Select the disk*

14. Specify size of the volume (see Figure 3-15).

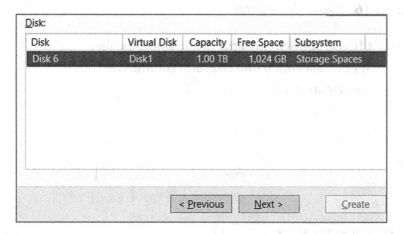

Figure 3-15. *Specify the size*

15. You can choose to assign the volume as a drive or a folder (see Figure 3-16).

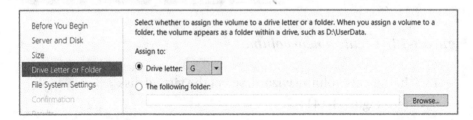

Figure 3-16. *Select drive letter*

16. Choose File System Settings and select the file system, allocation unit size, and volume label (see Figure 3-17).

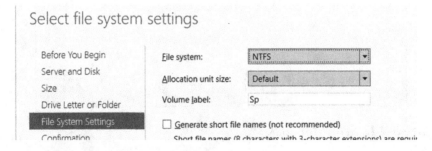

Figure 3-17. *File system settings*

17. Confirm the volume information and create the volume (see Figure 3-18).

Confirm that the following are the correct settings, and then click Create.

VOLUME LOCATION

Server:	Demowebvm1
Subsystem:	Storage Spaces
Virtual disk:	Disk1
Disk:	Disk 6
Free space:	1,024 GB

VOLUME PROPERTIES

Volume size:	1,024 GB
Drive letter or folder:	G:\
Volume label:	Sp

FILE SYSTEM SETTINGS

File system:	NTFS
Short file name creation:	Disabled
Allocation unit size:	Default

Figure 3-18. *Volume details*

Although not a feature-to-feature mapping, you can get functionalities like RAID 0 and RAID 1 in Azure using features such as storage replication at the platform layer and storage spaces at the VM layer.

Storage for Compute

When planning for VM storage in Azure, the estimated data size and performance requirements are of prime importance.

VM Data Size

The size of the data that is expected to be stored in a VM plays an important role when selecting the VM instance type. The maximum number of data disks that can be supported by the SKU is fixed. If the VM needs more disks to be added at any point in its life cycle, then the only option is to scale up the VM, which may result in application downtime. The cost also depends on the size of the disk provisioned. If using an unmanaged standard disk, you pay only for the data stored in the disk. In all other cases (i.e., managed or unmanaged premium disks), the cost of the data is fixed and chargeable according to the provisioned disk size; hence, over-provisioning of storage, such as a premium disk, could result in unwanted cloud charges

VM Disk Performance

The standard disk can provide only 500 input/output operations per second (IOPS) per disk, which may not be sufficient for high-IO intensive applications. Premium disks offer higher IOPS levels and are recommended for production workloads, especially read/write–intensive ones. Azure commits a single VM SLA of 99.9% if all the disks associated with the VM use premium storage. For VMs using standard disks, a minimum of two VMs in an availability set is required to get the committed SLA.

File Services

Azure file share allows you to create server message block (SMB) -based file shares in Azure storage. These file shares can be mapped on to any SMB 3.0–supported servers on-premise or hosted in Azure. For VMs hosted in Azure, this service can be leveraged by server operating systems starting at Windows Server 2008 R2 and client operating systems starting at Windows 7. For machines hosted on-premise, Azure files are supported starting at Windows Server 2012 for server OS and Windows 8.1 for client OS.

Azure file share is mounted by providing the Azure storage account key as credentials. SMB port 445 should be opened in the firewall in environments with network restrictions. Azure file share is considered equivalent to the NAS-based file shares on-premise. The only difference is that you implement username/password–based fine-grained access control.

A new service called Azure File Sync is in preview. It syncs file shares in Azure with file shares in your on-premise server to provide a hybrid solution. It also helps in disaster recovery scenario, where in the event of an on-premise machine failure, the File Sync service can be installed on a new server to resync the data.

Hybrid Storage: StorSimple

Azure StorSimple is Microsoft's offering in the hybrid cloud storage space. It is capable of catering to all key storage requirements, such as primary storage, data archival, tape replacement, intelligent tiering, offsite storage, and so forth. It has automatic storage tiering and can tier all lesser-used and archival data to Azure cloud storage without any operational overhead. This cloud-integrated storage mechanism was developed by a company called StorSimple, which was acquired by Microsoft. It is offered under the Azure Hybrid Cloud storage solution umbrella.

The following are some of the key features of this storage solution:

- Seamless integration of cloud storage with local storage

- Automated tiering mechanism

- Combination of SAS and SSD drives for local storage

- Deduplication and compression of data

- Thin provisioning

- Local snapshots and cloud snapshots for backup

- Certified support from VMware

- Built-in resiliency for hardware devices with dual controller; hot swappable

- Non-disruptive software upgrade

- Integrated DR capabilities for recovery from cloud storage

- Deterministic thin restores to download only the working data set

Now let's look at StorSimple devices, which are available as physical rack mountable storage devices, virtual appliances, or cloud appliances.

StorSimple Physical Devices: 8100 and 8600 Models

There are two models: the 8100 series and the 8600 series. 8100 is a 2U device with 15 TB total usable local capacity of and 200 TB maximum capacity, including cloud storage. 8600 is a 4U device with an *extended bunch of disks* (EBOD) enclosure and related components. It has 40 TB total usable local capacity and 500 TB maximum capacity, including cloud storage. The storage enclosures include a combination of SSD and HDD drives for local storage. There are 12 disk drive slots per enclosure. 8600 devices have an additional 12 slots in the EBOD enclosure. The drive slots support SAS disk drives, which can be a combination of SSD and HDD. The devices have built-in resiliency, with share processors and storage along with mirrored controllers in active-passive mode.

StorSimple Cloud Appliance: 8010 and 8020 Models

The StorSimple cloud appliance runs in Azure as a virtual machine. In the Microsoft StorSimple documentation, you may find it referred to as the StorSimple virtual device. It comes in two models: 8010 and 8020. The 8010 devices can support a maximum capacity of 30 TB, and the 8020 devices support up to 64 TB. The 8020 is the latest model and has the capability to support premium storage for high-performance workloads. You can connect volumes exposed by the StorSimple cloud appliance to your virtual machines in Azure using iSCSI protocol.

Disaster recovery (DR) is another important target use case for cloud appliances. You can failover from your physical StorSimple device to a cloud appliance in the event of a disaster and bring up your machines in the cloud.

Note   The StorSimple cloud appliance is always used in conjunction with a StorSimple physical appliance. One of the prerequisites of using a StorSimple cloud appliance is that you should have a physical device registered with the StorSimple manager service running from the Azure portal.

StorSimple Virtual Array: 1200 Model

The StorSimple virtual array is an OVA format of the StorSimple physical device. It can be deployed both in VMware and Hyper-V hypervisors. It provides 6.4 TB maximum local storage capacity of and has total capacity of up to 64 TB, including cloud storage. This solution targets enterprises that want a cost-effective but hybrid cloud-based storage solution. It supports volumes exposed as iSCSI targets, along with SMB/CIFS-based file shares.

In terms of management and confirmation, you can use it the same way that you would use a physical StorSimple device. There are certain limitations when compared to the physical device, however. For example, it has lower storage capacity, including cloud storage (i.e., 64 TB) than the 200 TB or 500 TB supported by the 8100 and 8600 devices, respectively. Also, being a virtual device, the performance is dependent on the underlying infra and virtualization platform. However, it supports all major use cases, such as cloud-based storage, backup, and disaster recovery. It can also be registered and managed from the Azure portal.

Let's explore some of the key features of StorSimple.

Automatic Tiering

StorSimple uses three layers of storage: SSD, HDD, and cloud storage. The read and write of fresh data always happens in the SSD tier. When data gets aged and is accessed less, it is tiered to the HDD layer. The cold data (i.e., the least accessed data) is tiered to the Azure cloud storage tier. With this architecture, organizations need not worry about local storage capacity management and planning, since cloud storage is integrated with the solution and archival data is automatically tiered to it.

When data is first written to the device, it goes to the SSD tier. Inline deduplication and compression is active, but the archival procedure doesn't kick in until much later. So, the data continues to be written in this tier until a defined low-threshold limit and a high threshold are reached. At this point, the system starts identifying the non-working set of data (i.e., the oldest data), which is spilled over to the next tier (i.e., HDD).

Lower and higher thresholds are always kept empty because we want to keep some buffer space available if the user ever wants to restore archival data. The threshold limit is 94% for 8000 series, after which data is migrated from SSD to HDD and from HDD to Azure Storage. These processes are transparent to users and applications, and there is no impact on how they access the data (see Figure 3-19).

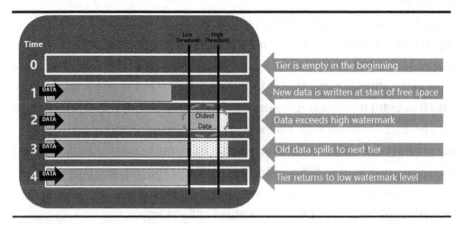

Figure 3-19. *Automated tiering*

In a StorSimple virtual array, there is no concept of SSD and HDD tiers; hence, the data is tiered directly to the cloud from the local storage (i.e., the virtual hard disk). It is done based on a data heat map, which tracks data usage, its age, and its relationship with other data. The active data, or hot data, is stored locally, and cold /inactive data is tiered to cloud storage.

Deduplication, Compression, and Encryption

Deduplication is enabled by default in StorSimple devices, and there are no special licenses associated with it. When data comes into a StorSimple device, it is written in 64 KB blocks. For every block, hash keys are built, and a metadata map is created. The SSD tier consists of raw storage and the metadata map. Deduplication happens in the SSD layer, thereby ensuring performance. When data comes in, it is matched with the metadata map. If a block exists, it is discarded, and the pointers are updated. This is the same as data being read. It helps in optimal utilization of local capacity and makes operations like data migrations time efficient.

As mentioned, data spills over to the HDD layer once the high watermark is reached in the SSD tier. Lossless compression of data sets is done in the HDD tier. Deflate compression is used, which means that data residing in the HDD tier is fully deduped and compressed. However, users can continue to access the data in the device without any noticeable difference, because the entire process is transparent.

When data is tiered out from StorSimple array local storage to the cloud, it is encrypted using AES-256 encryption. The customer holds the encrypted data. Data is converted to iSCSI blocks, deduped, compressed, and then encrypted before sending to Azure. The data is sent to Azure over HTTPS. Data residing in Azure is further protected by role-based access control (RBAC) mechanisms, the log in password, auditing, access keys, and so forth. These are StorSimple's different layers of security for your data.

To summarize the process, deduplication happens in the SSD tier, and when SSD reaches capacity, the data is compressed and moved to the HDD tier. When the data is ready to be tiered to the cloud, it is encrypted and sent to cloud storage over HTTPS. However, in a virtual array, there is a small difference wherein the data that resides in the local storage is not deduplicated and compressed. The deduplication, compression, and encryption happen before data is tiered to cloud storage.

Local Snapshots and Cloud Snapshots

Snapshots refer to the built-in backup mechanism in StorSimple devices. There are two types of backups: local snapshots and cloud snapshots. Local snapshots are point-in-time copies of data in StorSimple local storage. They are usually scheduled on a daily and a weekly basis with shorter retention periods. They are useful for restoring any recently deleted data. Local snapshots use the Copy Reference on Write (CROW) method. It makes use of volume metadata references for creating storage-efficient snapshots, and it is stored locally in the devices.

Cloud snapshots are point-in-time copies of data in Azure cloud storage. Cloud snapshots are typically scheduled with longer retention periods, like weeks and months, and are useful in DR scenarios. In cloud snapshots, the data and metadata are copied over to the cloud when the snapshot is taken for the first time. All subsequent snapshots are incremental (i.e., only the changed data and metadata is copied over to cloud, thereby optimizing the cloud storage usage).

StorSimple physical array supports both local and cloud snapshots. However Virtual array supports only Cloud snapshots.

Third-Party Solutions

Third-party vendors provide storage solutions that integrate with Azure storage to enable robust hybrid cloud architecture. For example, vendors like NetAPP, Cohesity, and Commvault provide tools for single pane management of data on-premise and in the cloud. If the organization has an existing investment with a storage vendor, it can check for availability of a hybrid cloud storage solution from the same vendor that integrates with Azure. For example, NetAPP's ONTAP cloud helps manage and deploy storage virtual appliances in Azure. These virtual appliances can be used to create iSCSI targets and file shares in Azure, such as on-premise storage systems.

Designing Secure Networks

When migrating workloads to Azure, the following aspects should be factored:

- Network segmentation
- Allowed and denied communication between networks
- Expected traffic flow
- Traffic monitoring

The best practices for implementing network layer security are explained in Chapter 7. This chapter focuses on the design aspects of the network.

VLANs and VNets

Let's start with a simple on-premise network architecture. The environment has a DMZ and an internal network in place (see Figure 3-20). The traffic reached DMZ via a firewall so that only incoming traffic at port 443 or port 80 is allowed in the network. Only traffic from the DMZ network is allowed to the internal network. There is a defined traffic flow within the network, where only the web server can communicate with application server, and only the application server can communicate with the DB server.

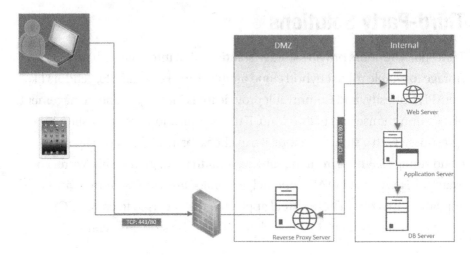

Figure 3-20. *On-premise architecture*

Note   It is important to understand that the Azure network configuration works at Layer 3, and there is no VLAN equivalent service. Azure provides a VNet with network segregation. In an on-premise environment, the network defined in Figure 3-20 could be part of a VLAN. When we migrate it to Azure, however, the segmentation should be achieved via VNets.

In Azure, this network layer isolation is achieved via VNets and subnets. The traffic restrictions between the layers can be achieved through different options, such as NSGs, address spaces, user-defined routing, and even third-party virtual network appliances if required. The VNet creation process is covered in Chapter 1. Here we investigate some of the important VNet settings and how they map to on-premise architecture components.

The virtual network Overview tab provides generic information on the virtual network, the resource group name, subscription details, address space, and connected devices (see Figure 3-21).

Figure 3-21. *VNet overview*

The activity log tag provides information on any admin activities associated with the virtual network and its status (i.e., error, warning, critical, or informational) (see Figure 3-22).

Figure 3-22. *Activity log*

Access control (IAM) provides fine-grain control over VNet management permissions. You can add/remove administrative users or apps from this window (see Figure 3-23).

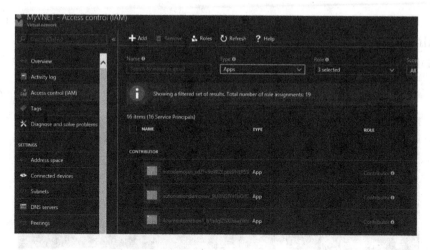

Figure 3-23. *Access control*

You can also add tags for ease of management and billing administration. Tags are essentially key-value pairs that can be added to any Azure resource. Resources can be sorted based on the allocated tags for logical grouping. Tags are also reflected in the detailed billing CSV, which helps identify charges incurred by all resources categorized under a specific tag (see Figure 3-24).

Figure 3-24. *Tags*

The address space is the range of IP addresses available for allocation within a VNet. They are private IP address ranges that can be defined in CIDR (Classless Inter-Domain Routing) format from VNet settings (see Figure 3-25).

Figure 3-25. *VNet address space*

You can carve out subnets from the defined address space by providing the address range (CIDR block). Any network security groups or route tables can be attached during subnet creation. Ideally, the different application tiers like web, app, DB, and so forth, should be placed in different subnets as a design best practice. You can also enable service endpoints for Azure services such as storage and Azure SQL. Service endpoints enable private connections to these services, rather than the default public connectivity option. This offers a more secure way to connect to resources in Azure (see Figure 3-26).

Figure 3-26. Subnet details

Configure the DNS server settings. You can either use the DNS provided by Azure or provide a different IP as the DNS. All the virtual machines connected to the network use this IP as the DNS server. This configuration is useful if you want to set up an Active Directory domain inside the Azure VNet. In that use case, the IP of the AD server should be provided as the DNS server. If the VNet is connected to an on-premise environment via VPN, you might want to give the private IP address your on-premise AD here (see Figure 3-27).

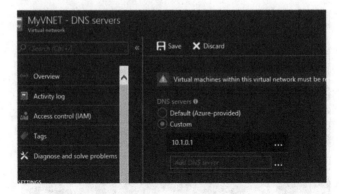

Figure 3-27. DNS configuration

You can also configure a VNet peering to connect the VNets in the same Azure region without using any VPN gateways. The traffic in this case flows through the Azure network backbone. This setting is beneficial for customers with resources in multiple VNets and want them to communicate with each other without incurring the cost of a VPN gateway (see Figure 3-28).

Figure 3-28. *VNet peering*

To secure the network from an administrative perspective, you can create locks at the VNet level; for example, you can create a lock to prevent deletion. You can also create a read-only lock so that all authorized users have only read-level access unless the lock is deleted (see Figure 3-29).

Figure 3-29. *Network locks*

IPAM, DHCP, and DNS

Every machine created in Azure has a private IP address allocated to it from the back-end DHCP (Dynamic Host Configuration Protocol) service. The range of the IP address is defined by the subnet CIDR. In every subnet, the first four IP addresses are reserved by Azure, and the remaining IPs are dynamically allocated to virtual machines. You can make these IP addresses static from the portal or via PowerShell. You can convert an IP from dynamic to static and vice versa from the VM's NIC card settings. Navigate to the VM and select **Networking ➤ NIC card ➤ IP configurations** (see Figure 3-30).

Figure 3-30. IP configuration

In addition to NIC cards, private IPs can be assigned to load balancers and application gateways.

Public IPs can be assigned to Internet-facing endpoints like VMs, VPN gateways, Internet-facing load balancers, and application gateways. Like private IPs, this allocation is dynamic by default and can be converted to static from the portal.

The only difference is that you cannot change the allocated public IP to an IP of your choice, because it is allocated from an Azure pool of public IP addresses. However, you can convert the allocated IP to static and reserve it for a resource throughout its life cycle. Public IP addresses are independent resources in Azure Resource Manager and can be managed directly from the Azure portal. From the Azure portal, select the public IP addresses. Select the IP and make changes from **Settings ➤ Configuration** (see Figure 3-31).

Figure 3-31. *Public IP configuration*

DNS resolution is important in any network, including Azure VNets. The DNS configuration is explained in the previous section. Azure has a built-in multitenant DNS service that provides DNS resolutions for all the attached virtual machines in a network. However, this service also has certain limitations. You cannot register your own DNS records, and it is not WINS or NETBIOS compatible. These features are required in a majority of production scenarios, and hence customers can choose a custom DNS that allows these features. When using a custom DNS, you can still leverage the Azure-provided DNS service for all recursive queries by sending them to IP 168.63.129.16.

User-Defined Routing

The different routing mechanisms in Azure were explained in Chapter 1. Here we focus on the configuration of user-defined routes that enable you to change the default traffic flow.

Search for "route tables" in the Azure portal, and click **Add** to create the new route table. Provide basic information, such as the resource group name, subscription, and location. Add a new route from **Settings ➤ Routes**. Provide a route name, the address prefix of the destination network in CIDR format, and the next hop type. If you are planning to redirect the traffic to a virtual network appliance, then the appliance's IP should also be provided in this window. The VM acting as a virtual network appliance should also have IP forwarding enabled for this configuration to work (see Figure 3-32).

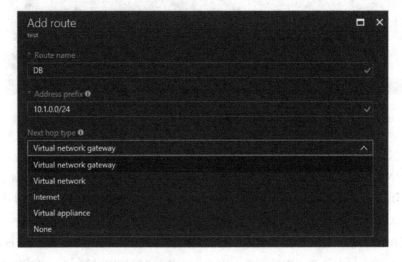

Figure 3-32. Add route

Network Security Groups

Network security groups (NSGs) provide basic incoming and outgoing traffic management capabilities. You can restrict the incoming traffic to a specific IP and port. Filtering can also be done based on the source IP address/CIDR range. The same can be applied to outgoing traffic. By default, all outbound traffic is enabled in an Azure VM. However, if you want to restrict this traffic, create and attach a specific NSG to the VM NIC card so that only the defined traffic is allowed outbound. It is important to note, however, that NSGs do not have any traffic routing capabilities. They provide simple network filtering capabilities. They can be considered as replacement of on-premise firewalls with basic functionalities from a migration standpoint.

Note   NSGs are discussed in detail in Chapter 7.

On-Prem vs. Azure: Sample Architecture Comparison

The on-premise architecture that you saw earlier in the chapter can be transformed to an Azure architecture, as shown in Figure 3-33.

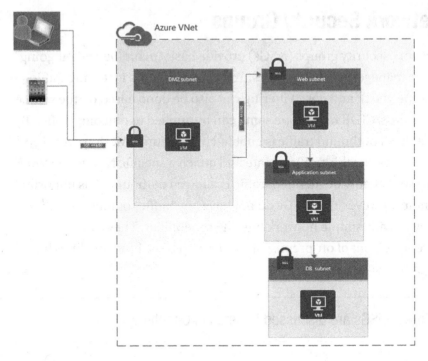

Figure 3-33. *Azure sample architecture*

As you can see in the architecture, NSGs can replace the firewall to filter the incoming traffic. The DMZ network and application tiers can be configured in different subnets, again with attached NSGs to allow only the required traffic to traverse. Thus, all the required restrictions allowed in the original architecture can be achieved in Azure as well.

Summary

This chapter compared on-premise storage and network components to what is available in Azure. The Azure components were explored in detail to provide insights on their functionalities.

CHAPTER 4

Implement Scalable Infrastructure in Azure

One of the key highlights of a cloud environment is the ability to scale resources on a demand basis and pay only for what is being used. This chapter focuses on the design considerations and configuration options to scale up or scale out environments hosted in Azure.

Scale up vs. Scale Out

Vertical scaling, or scale up, is the scenario in which the compute capacity of VMs is increased by switching the instance SKUs to a higher spec version when there is a surge in resource utilization (for example, during peak hours). The VMs can later be resized to smaller size, or scaled down, during off-peak hours.

Scale out, or horizontal scaling, uses Virtual Machine Scale Sets (VMSS). It works by adding more VMs from a predefined spec to support the application workload during peak hours. Scaling can be triggered automatically by predefined metrics such as CPU/ memory utilization, free disk space, and so forth, or based on a predefined schedule. The additional VMs are automatically scaled in once the resource utilization is lower or based on the schedule.

© Shijimol Ambi Karthikeyan 2018
S. Ambi Karthikeyan, *Practical Microsoft Azure IaaS*,
https://doi.org/10.1007/978-1-4842-3763-2_4

The decision to scale up or scale out depends on several factors and capabilities available in the Azure platform. Here are some of the key points to be considered:

- To rein in the ongoing costs of running applications on VMs, the VMs can be scaled down to a minimum spec during weekends, holidays, or off-peak hours.

- During vertical scaling, VMs are resized, which causes downtime to the hosted application. To avoid this, the architecture should be designed for high availability using Azure load balancers, availability sets, or availability zones.

- Scaling up is the preferred option for stateful applications. Scaling out with VM scale sets is recommended for stateless applications.

Scale up Azure Virtual Machines

After creating Azure virtual machines, they can be scaled up based on the available VM SKUs in a given region.

You can do the scaling from the virtual machine's settings by selecting the Size option (see Figure 4-1).

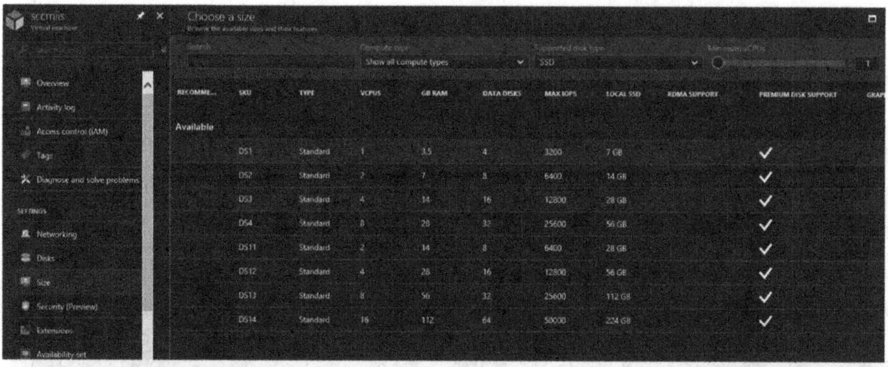

Figure 4-1. *Select VM SKU*

By changing the filters on the top, you can choose from the available
list of VMs. You can set filters for the compute types, or search for a specific
VM SKU by its name (see Figure 4-2).

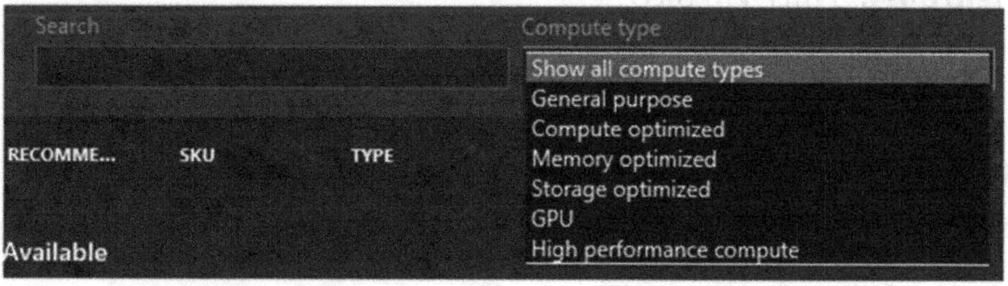

Figure 4-2. *VM SKU search options*

You can also refine the filter based on the hard disk type that is
required (i.e., SSD or HDD (see Figure 4-3).

Figure 4-3. *Hard disk and vCPU configuration*

Consider a use case where the customer is using a general-purpose VM but realizes after monitoring the VM utilization metrics that they need a memory-optimized VM for better performance. In that case, the filter can be set as shown in Figure 4-4 to choose from an available memory-optimized VM SKU. Select the option from the drop-down list and choose from the available SKUs.

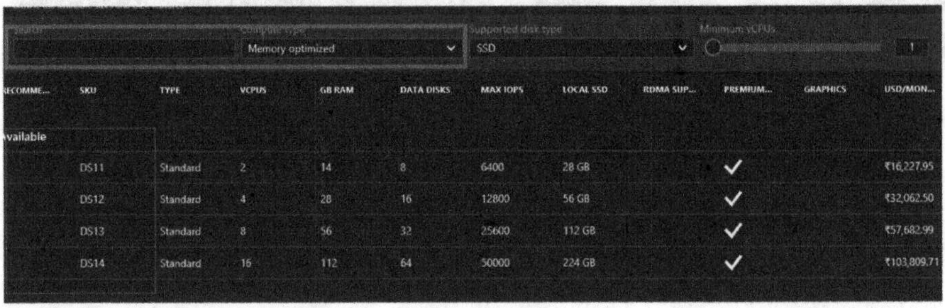

RECOMME...	SKU	TYPE	VCPUS	GB RAM	DATA DISKS	MAX IOPS	LOCAL SSD	RDMA SUP...	PREMIUM...	GRAPHICS	USD/MON...
Available											
	DS11	Standard	2	14	8	6400	28 GB		✓		₹16,227.95
	DS12	Standard	4	28	16	12800	56 GB		✓		₹32,062.50
	DS13	Standard	8	56	32	25600	112 GB		✓		₹57,682.99
	DS14	Standard	16	112	64	50000	224 GB		✓		₹103,809.71

Figure 4-4. *Filter VM SKU*

Note that the list also provides additional information about the specs of the available instance types (i.e., vCPU, memory, data disks, maximum IOPs, size of local SSD, graphic card, support, etc.). Choose the target VM type, and click **Select** (see Figure 4-5).

Figure 4-5. *Select VM SKU*

The VM is resized and you get the notification shown in Figure 4-6.

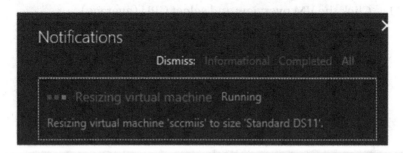

Figure 4-6. *Notification*

There is downtime involved during the process, and the machine is restarted in the new SKU. You can see the status in the Overview page, where the new VM SKU is reflected (see Figure 4-7).

Figure 4-7. *VM status*

Scale up Using Automation Runbooks

Azure Automation runbooks can enable the scale up of virtual machines. The metrics associated with the VMs can trigger a runbook to scale a VM to the next available size.

The VM basic metrics are available in the Overview pane of the VM. Note that these metrics are the host VM metrics, which are available in the Azure portal without any additional configuration. To make detailed guest/OS metrics available, the diagnostics extension should be enabled in the VM. In this sample walkthrough, we use CPU percentage as metrics, which are available by default.

1. Click the VM overview and select CPU (average) (see Figure 4-8).

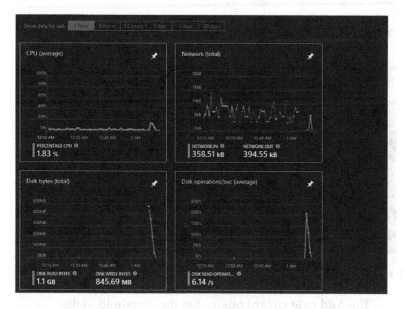

Figure 4-8. *VM Metrics*

2. Make sure that the correct metrics are selected,
    which in this case is Host Percentage CPU. Select the
    Add metrics alert (classic) option on the top to add
    the alert and configure the web hook. Please note
    that there is also a metrics experience available in
    the portal at the time of authoring this book, but in
    preview mode (see Figure 4-9).

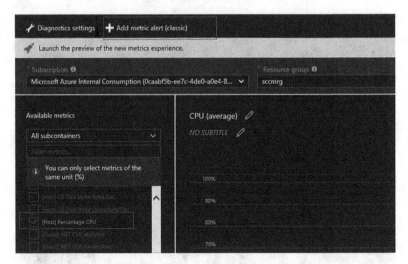

Figure 4-9. *Add metric alert*

3. The **Add rule** wizard opens. Set the threshold to the
   desired value. In this example, the value is set to 80%
   Host CPU percentage (see Figure 4-10).

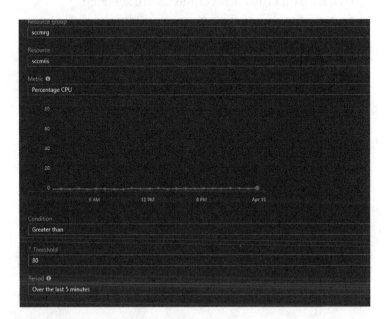

Figure 4-10. *CPU utilization threshold*

4. You can either choose to run an automation runbook or call a logic app when the alert is triggered (see Figure 4-11). Choose the **Run a runbook from this alert** option.

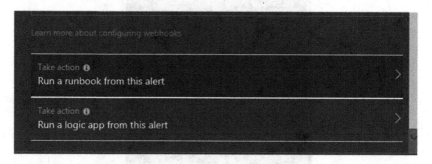

Figure 4-11. Take action

5. Under the Configure Runbook option, enable the runbook and choose the config source as either built-in or user. If you select the User option, you choose from a runbook that you created in your automation account. If you select the Built-in option, a list of runbooks is presented in a drop-down menu. Choose **Scale Up VM** to resize the VM to the next larger size (see Figure 4-12).

Figure 4-12. *Select runbook*

6. Choose the automation account for the runbook
    (see Figure 4-13).

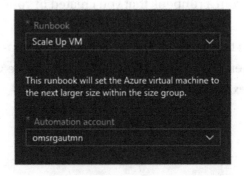

Figure 4-13. *Choose automation account*

7. Click OK in the **Add rule** wizard to complete the
    configuration (see Figure 4-14).

Figure 4-14. *Add rule*

Scale out Using VMSS

VMSS can scale VMs on a demand basis so that hosted applications can use up to 1000 VMs to meet peak usage demands. The VMs are behind a load balancer to evenly distribute the workload. The VM scale out and scale in is transparent to the end customer, and it is executed based on the defined scaling metrics.

- VMSS is a set of virtual machines of the same spec. Configuration is created from an Azure Marketplace image or an image uploaded by the customer.

- The network configurations are automatically taken care of when new instances are added.

- A public-facing load balancer is automatically created when the VMSS is provisioned. It is used for Layer 4 load balancing. An application gateway can also be linked to a VMSS for Layer 7 load balancing.

- VM scaling is based on metrics or on a schedule.

- By integrating VMSS with Azure Automation, you can also vertically scale VMs in VMSS within a certain range of Azure VMs.

Create VMSS

Let's get started.

1. Search for "virtual machine scale" in **All services** on the Azure dashboard (see Figure 4-15).

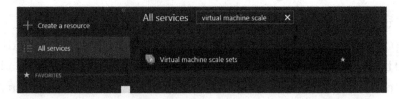

Figure 4-15. *Search for VMSS*

2.   Click **Add** to create a new scale set (see Figure 4-16).

Figure 4-16. Add new scale set

3.   In the **Create virtual machine scale set** wizard,
     enter basic information such as the name of the
     scale Set, the OS image to be used, the resource
     group, location, and the availability zone if
     applicable (see Figure 4-17).

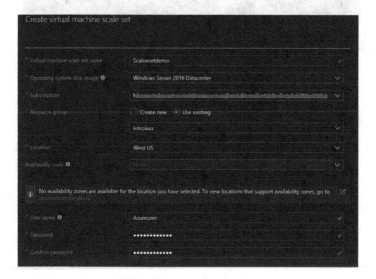

Figure 4-17. Basic configuration

4. Enter the VMSS configuration information
    (see Figure 4-18).

Figure 4-18. *VMSS configuration details*

5. Enter the number of instances for the scale set and
    the instance size.

6. Enter the instance size from the drop-down list.

7. Choose either managed disk or unmanaged disk. If
    you use unmanaged disk, the number of VMs in a
    scale set is limited to 100 VMs.

8. Provide a public IP address name and a unique
    domain name label.

9. Enable Autoscale and configure the minimum and
    maximum number of VMs allowed in the scale set.

10. Configure the CPU threshold and the number of
    VMs to be added or removed from the scale set
    based on the CPU threshold.

11. Click **Create** to create the virtual machine.

Configure VMSS

Once the scale set is created, additional configurations can be made from
the VMSS settings.

1. To view the number of instances, go to **VMSS ➤**
   Settings ➤ Instances (see Figure 4-19).

Figure 4-19. *VMSS instances*

2. To modify the scaling logic, go to **VMSS ➤ Settings**
   ➤ Scaling. You can edit the default scaling rule, or
   click **Add a Scale condition** to add new scaling rule
   (see Figure 4-20).

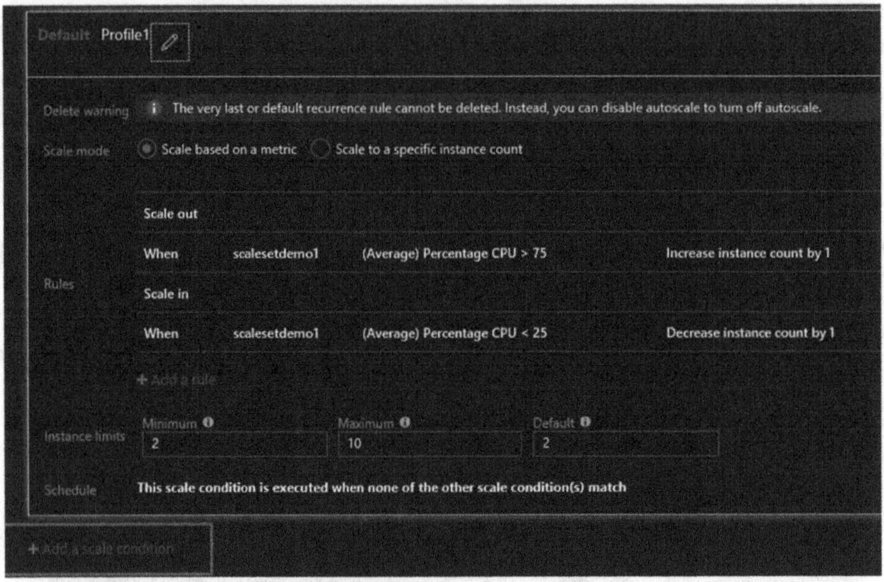

Figure 4-20. *Add a scale condition*

3. Select **Scale based on a metric** to set another
    scale rule based on VM metrics (or choose **Scale
    to a specific instance count** to scale based on a
    schedule). Click **Add a rule** (see Figure 4-21).

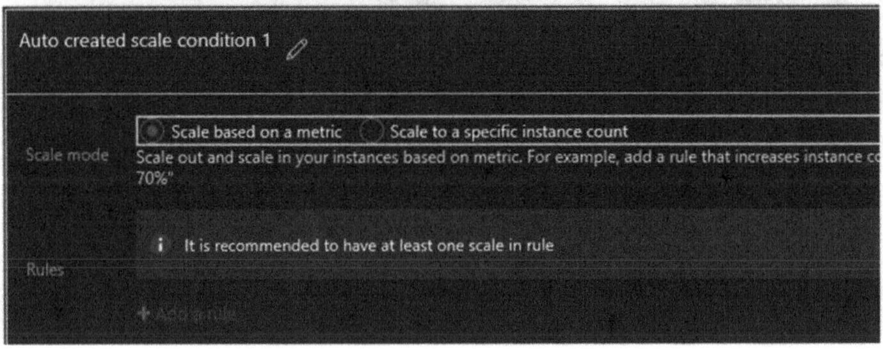

Figure 4-21. *Add scaling rule*

4. Select the metrics (see Figure 4-22).

Figure 4-22. *Select metric name*

5. Configure the threshold and the scaling operation
    (see Figure 4-23).

Figure 4-23. *Threshold settings*

6. The cool down period configured is the time to
    wait for the scaling to happen again after a scale
    operation (i.e., add more instances if required.
    Similarly, a scale in rule should be added to
    reduce the number of instances once the resource
    utilization falls below the metric. You can also add
    a start date and an end date for these metrics (see
    Figure 4-24).

Figure 4-24. *Schedule scaling period*

7. Click **Save** to update the Autoscale settings.

8. The size of the instances in the scale set can be
    changed manually from the portal. Go to the
    provisioned **VMSS ➤ Settings ➤ Size** and choose a
    different VM SKU (see Figure 4-25).

Figure 4-25. *Change VM SKU*

9. VM connectivity is through a public-facing load
    balancer that is automatically created during
    VMSS provisioning. You can view the inbound NAT
    settings to the VMSS member VMs by selecting the
    associated load balancer. Go to **Resource group**
    and select the load balancer. It is usually created
    using the naming convention <scalesetname>lb.
    The VMSS member VMs is added to the back-end
    pool of the load balancer. You can see the back-end
    pool members from **Load balancer ➤ Settings ➤
    Backend pools** (see Figure 4-26).

Figure 4-26. *Back-end pool*

10. A default load balancing rule is also created for port
    80 of the load balancer, redirecting traffic to port 80
    of the backend VM pools. Based on the application
    requirements, you can edit this rule directly from
    the portal (see Figure 4-27).

Figure 4-27. *Load balancing rule*

11. The associated health probe can be edited from
     Load balancer ➤ Settings ➤ Health probes
     (see Figure 4-28).

Figure 4-28. Health probe

12. In the settings, click **Inbound NAT rules** to view the
     NAT rules that allow RDP connection (see Figure 4-29).

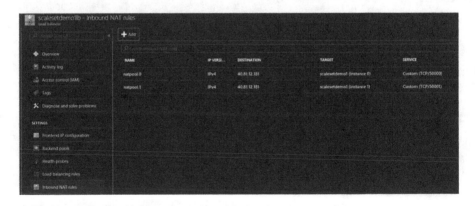

Figure 4-29. NAT rule

13. With Windows VMSS, port 50000 is mapped to
     the RDP port of the first machine in the scale set.
     Port 500001 is mapped to the RDP port of the next
     machine, and so on (see Figure 4-30).

Figure 4-30. *NAT rule port mapping*

Note   At the time of writing this book, the default NAT rules cannot
be edited from the portal.

Scalability at Storage and Networking Layers

Azure Storage is highly available and scalable by design. The scalability targets of Azure Storage are well defined in Azure product documentation and should be carefully reviewed before making any design decisions. If the usage exceeds the defined limits, Azure Storage throws error codes like 503 (server busy) or 500 (operation timeout). Scalability becomes a deciding factor in IaaS particularly when designing large environments using unmanaged disks. In this case, it is important to consider factors such as the number of storage accounts per region, the maximum storage account capacity, the available IOPS at a given time, and so forth. However, you could also request that the Azure support team increase the default limits of storage, if required. For example, the default IOPS limit for a storage account is 20,000, which can be increased to 50,000 by raising a support request.

Networking scalability is also linked to the Azure subscription limits and is an important design consideration. The required number of virtual networks, VNet peerings, public IP addresses, user-defined routes, and so forth, should be analyzed against the subscription limits at the planning phase. The network bandwidth and the number of NICs that can be attached to a VM are dependent on the selected VM SKU. The network bandwidth is measured against egress traffic across all attached network interfaces. In some VM SKUs, you can enable accelerated networking to improve network performance. This configuration is done in new VMs using PowerShell or Azure CLI.

Summary

This chapter reviewed the scalability configurations available in Azure. Compute capacity can be scaled on the fly, either vertically or horizontally based on application requirements. It is more of a design decision and factors the right components when it comes to storage and network scalability.

CHAPTER 5

Design for Resiliency in Azure

Resilient environments are built by design for withstanding outages and hardware/software component failures. In Microsoft Azure, this is a joint responsibility where customers should leverage the platform features in their architecture to build a resilient environment. This chapter focuses on the distinctive features/components of Azure IaaS that build a resilient architecture.

Storage Layer Resiliency

VHDs used by VMs reside in back-end storage while using managed disks or unmanaged disks. Managed disks are recommended for resiliency because the underlying storage stamp is taken care of when the VMs are deployed in availability sets. The VM disks are distributed across fault domains and update domains just like compute instances. This ensures high availability and resiliency both at the compute layer and the storage layer.

With unmanaged disks, VMs can be placed in an availability set, and the disks of individual VMs can be placed in separate storage accounts. Availability sets ensure that the compute units are distributed across different fault domains and updated domains to avoid a single point of failure. The storage accounts used for hosting the VM disks come from

© Shijimol Ambi Karthikeyan 2018
S. Ambi Karthikeyan, *Practical Microsoft Azure IaaS*,
https://doi.org/10.1007/978-1-4842-3763-2_5

an underlying storage unit in Azure datacenters. There is no guarantee that the separate storage accounts that you use for your architecture is provisioned from a different storage unit. This architecture is depicted in Figure 5-1.

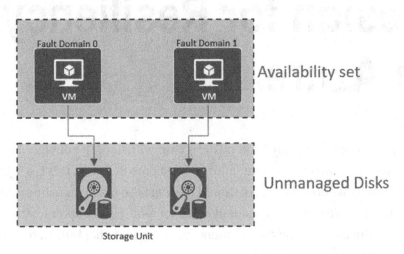

Figure 5-1. *Availability set with unmanaged disks*

When using managed disks for VMs, the concept of fault domains is extended to storage stamps as well. The storage account used for disks are determined by the platform. If VMs are distributed across availability sets, the platform intelligently places the disks associated with the VMs across multiple storage units or storage stamps. This ensures that not all VMs in the availability set are affected in the event of a failure in one storage unit (see Figure 5-2).

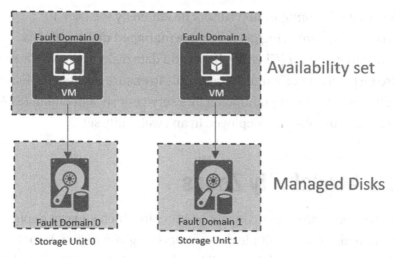

Figure 5-2. *Availability sets with managed disks*

From a configuration perspective, it is a straightforward process. When creating a VM from the portal, you can add it to an availability set in the **Configure optional features** option. If you have selected to use a managed disk, the availability set configuration is automatically aligned to it (see Figure 5-3).

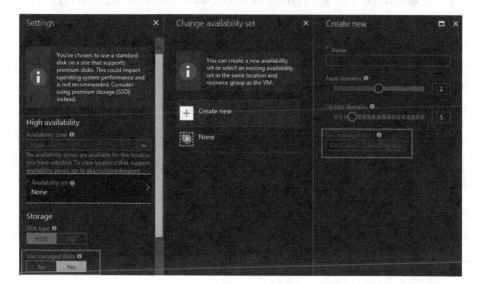

Figure 5-3. *Managed disks and availability set configuration in the portal*

Note that this configuration cannot be edited by the user. If unmanaged disks are being used, the **Use managed disks** option is automatically set to **No (Classic)**. If you add data disks to the VM later, they will also be placed in different storage units to ensure resiliency. Microsoft offers 99.95% availability guaranteed by a service-level agreement (SLA) when two or more VMs are deployed in an availability set.

Azure Availability Zones

Availability zones are a new concept in Azure in which you can deploy your workloads across multiple datacenters in a given region. Prior to availability sets, you could deploy VMs only in availability sets that placed the VMs in different hardware in a given datacenter.

There are a minimum of three availability zones in a given region. Each region acts as a fault domain consisting of different datacenters, thereby isolating single point of failures with independent power sources, cooling, and networking. Even if one of the datacenters in a given region is unavailable, the VM is still accessible from other datacenters in the availability zone, thereby providing resiliency against datacenter failures as well. In addition to VMs, services such as managed disks, load balancers, public IP addresses, zone-redundant storage, and SQL databases also support availability zones (see Figure 5-4).

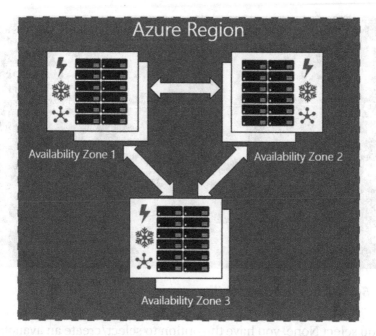

Figure 5-4. *Azure availability zone (image courtesy of Microsoft)*

At the time of writing this book, availability zones are generally
available in two regions: US Central and France Central. They are
available in preview in East US 2, West Europe, and Southeast Asia.
Availability zones can be configured while creating the virtual machine.
From the **Configure optional features** settings, choose either **Availability
zone** or **Availability set**. Select from one of the three availability zones in
the drop-down menu (see Figure 5-5).

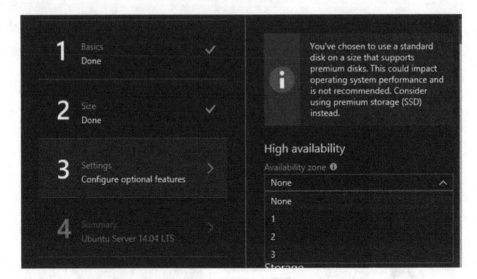

Figure 5-5. *Select the availability zone*

If you select None, you have the option to select/create an availability set (see Figure 5-6).

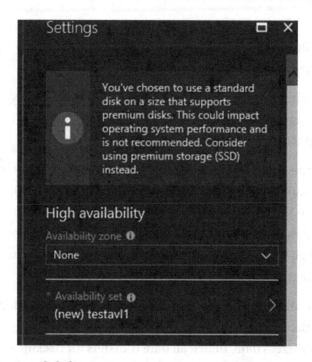

Figure 5-6. *Availability set*

Note   You can either use availability sets or availability zones, but not both for a VM.

VMs deployed in two or more availability zones in a region also have a financially backed SLA that guarantees availability to at least one instance 99.99% of the time.

Azure Backup Service for VMs, Files, and Applications

A well-defined backup plan for application and data is important in ensuring the resiliency of an infrastructure in Azure. Azure offers a native first-party solution called Azure Backup to address this requirement. Azure

Backup is available on a pay-as-you-go basis, which enables a solution economy while catering to enterprise backup needs. The following are some of the key benefits of this solution.

- The backup data is stored securely in Azure cloud storage, and hence there are no hassles of long-term capacity planning and management.

- Azure cloud storage used for backup data is resilient by default since it uses locally redundant storage (LRS). With LRS, three copies of your data exist within a region. If additional resiliency is needed, you can opt for globally redundant storage (GRS), which replicates data to a secondary paired region.

- There are no charges associated with restore operations or data egress during restore. Azure does not charge for ingress data, hence all data transfers for backup are effectively free.

- Data security is assured in transit and at rest. Data is encrypted using a passphrase managed by the customer.

- Unlike on-premise backup solutions with practical considerations for long-term data retention and storage, Azure Backup uses cloud storage and allows you to store data for longer periods. You can store 9999 recovery points for a protected instance at any given time. Depending on the configured recovery policies, you could store data for more than 100 years using the solution with guaranteed recovery. Long-term data retention is often required by organizations to meet certain compliance and regulatory standards.

- Azure Backup offers application-consistent backups that integrate with operating system components such as VSS to ensure that the data can be restored and used by applications without additional fixes.

Azure Backup Service Options

When your infrastructure is hosted in Azure, there are four options that you can choose from for backing up data and applications.

- **Azure Backup (MARS) agent**. This service is an independent agent that can be installed on a target backup machine to back up files, folders, and system states only.

- **Azure Backup (MAPS) server**. This service makes application-aware back up of workloads such as SQL, Exchange, and SharePoint, as well as files and folders. When used on-premise, it can also back up VMware and Hyper-V VMs. Unlike a backup agent, Azure Backup server allows centralized management of backup for multiple backup targets. It is the preferred solution for large-scale environment backup management.

- **System center DPM**. If your organization has an existing investment in a system center suite of products, you can integrate data protection manager (DPM) with Azure Backup by installing the backup agent. DPM and Azure Backup servers are functionally the same; Azure is built from the same code as DPM. The only difference is that when used on-premise, you cannot integrate tape drives with an Azure Backup server.

143

- **Azure VM backup**. This service allows you to make
platform-level backups of Azure VMs using the Azure
Backup service. The backup is done using the backup
extension that is installed in the VM. The extension
can integrate with VSS to make application-consistent
backups if the VM is up during backup. There is
flexibility in terms of restore, where you can either
restore the entire VM or map a drive of the VM and
copy files and folders from a restore point.

Azure Backup Initial Configuration

The Azure Recovery Services vault should be set up before you use any
backup option.

1. From the Azure portal dashboard, click **Create a
new resource ➤ Monitoring + Management ➤
Backup and Site Recovery (OMS)** (see Figure 5-7).

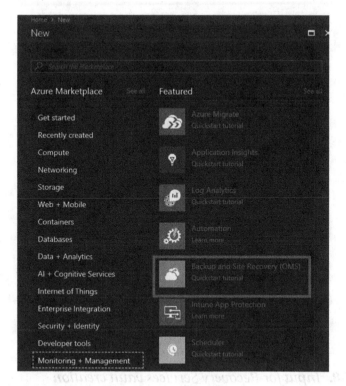

Figure 5-7. *Create Recovery Services vault*

2. Provide basic input information such as resource
   group, Recovery Services vault name, and location
   (see Figure 5-8).

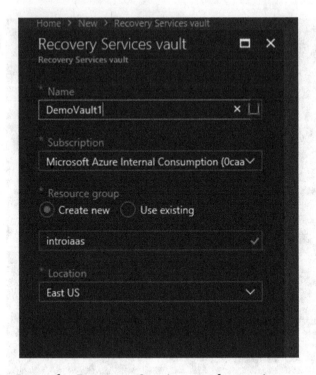

Figure 5-8. *Input for Recovery Services vault creation*

3. Select the backup goal in the Recovery Services
    vault. Open the backup vault that you created in the
    previous step. Go to **Get started ➤ Backup**. Select
    the use case for the Azure Backup agent, as shown in
    Figure 5-9.

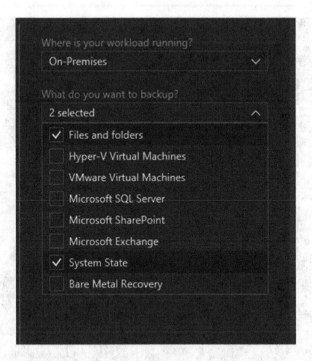

Figure 5-9. *MARS agent use case*

Note   Here we are focusing on making a backup from infrastructure in Azure. The options in the backup vault can be bit confusing because you need to select the On-Premises option and choose the workload. The steps are the same whether the workload is hosted in Azure or on-premise. In the On-Premises option, if you select only **Files and folders**, you still get the Azure Backup agent setup instructions.

---

4. Click **Prepare Infrastructure** and follow the instructions for installation and configuration of the backup agent (see Figure 5-10).

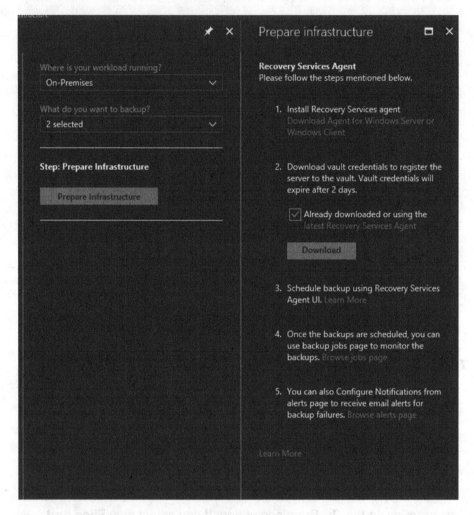

Figure 5-10. *MARS agent installation steps*

5. Download the backup agent that suits your client operating system.

6. The vault credentials can be downloaded at step 2, as shown in Figure 5-10. The credentials are required for registering the agent with the backup vault.

7. During on-premise agent installation, you have to generate a passphrase to encrypt the backup data (see Figure 5-11).

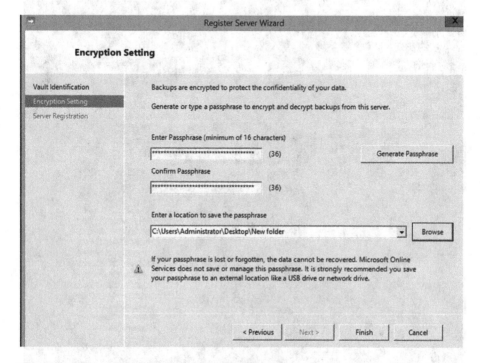

Figure 5-11. *MARS agent for passphrase*

Note   Make sure that the passphrase is stored on an external device or location. This passphrase is required if you want to recover the data by installing the agent on a different server in scenarios where the original machine crashes or is unavailable.

---

8. The backup server installation steps are provided when we select any advanced workload backup in the **Prepare infrastructure** wizard in the Recovery Services vault (see Figure 5-12).

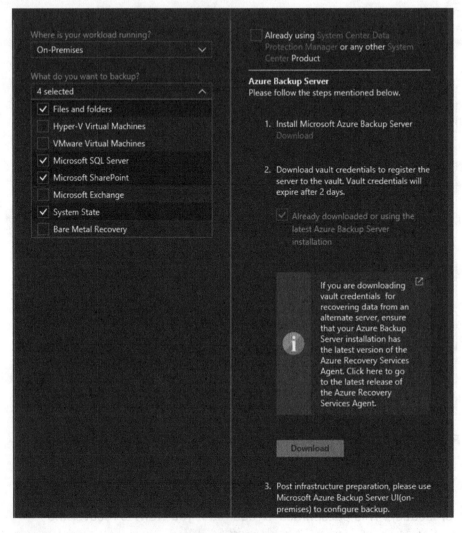

Figure 5-12. *Backup server use case and steps*

9. If you have a system center DPM license available,
    select the check box at the top to get the integration
    steps for DPM. The difference in the configuration is
    that after installing DPM, the recovery services agent
    should be installed to integrate it with Azure Backup

service. The steps are the same as an Azure Backup
agent installation, in which you need to provide the
vault credentials for registration and generate the
passphrase for encryption (see Figure 5-13).

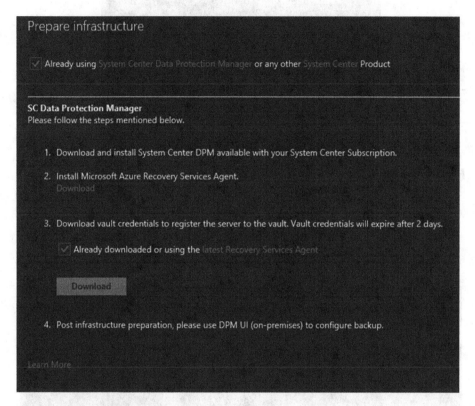

Figure 5-13. *DPM integration*

10. To take VM-level backup of virtual machines
hosted in Azure, select the following options in the
Recovery Services vault (see Figure 5-14).

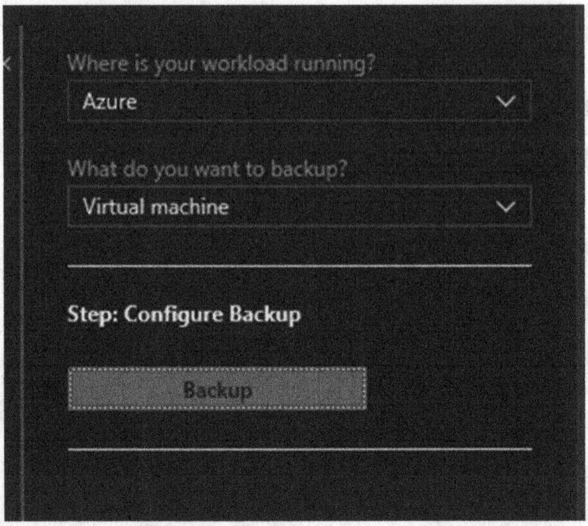

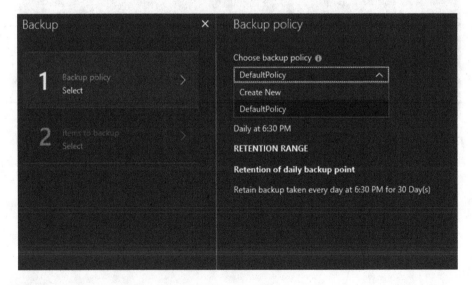

Figure 5-14. *Azure VM backup*

11. When you click Backup, the wizard takes you to the
option to use a default backup policy or create a new
backup policy (see Figure 5-15).

Figure 5-15. *Create a new backup policy*

Depending on your organization's data recovery, SLAs define the daily, weekly, monthly, and yearly retention points (see Figure 5-16). The following is a sample policy.

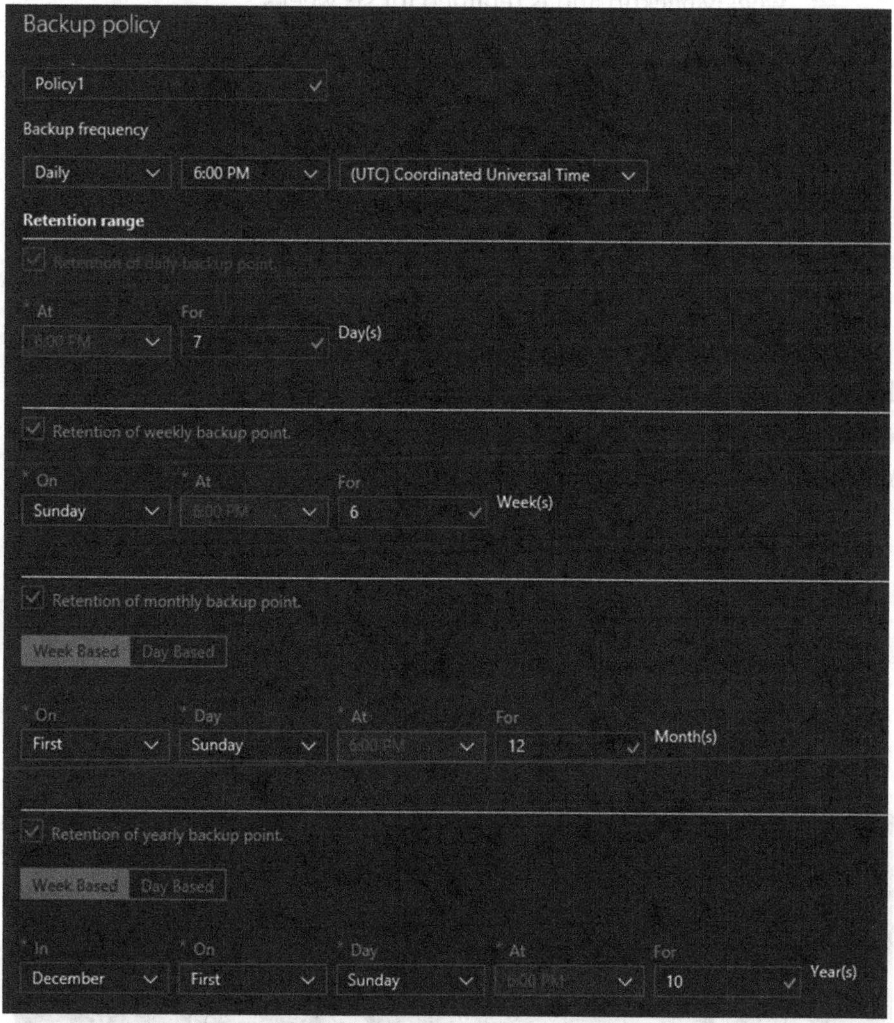

Figure 5-16. *Backup policy configuration*

- The backup is taken daily at 6:00 PM UTC.

- The daily backup point is retained for seven days.

- The backup taken on Sundays is considered as the weekly backup and is retained for six weeks.

- Backup taken on the first Sunday of every month is considered a monthly backup and is retained for 12 months.

- Backup taken on the first Sunday of December is considered the yearly backup and is stored for ten years from the day of backup.

Note that a similar backup policy configuration option is available in the backup agent, the Azure Backup server, and DPM from the respective tool interfaces. The policy configuration can be done directly from the Azure portal only for Azure VM backup.

12. The next step in VM backup is selecting the virtual machines that you want to backup. All VMs in the same geography as the backup vault for which backup is not currently enabled in any other vault are automatically listed in the wizard. Select the target VM and click OK (see Figure 5-17).

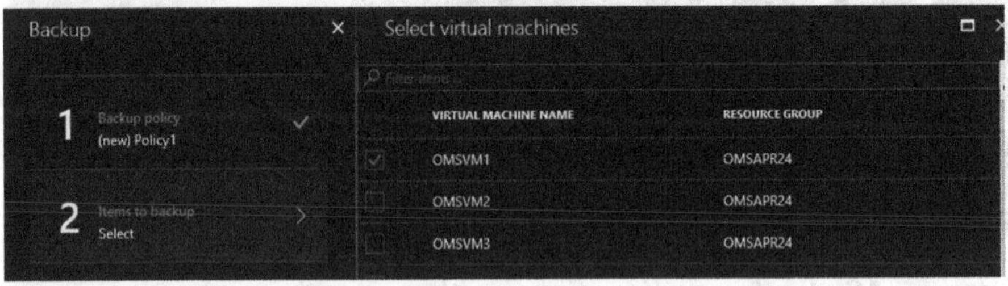

Figure 5-17. *Select target VMs*

13. For file and folder backup, the target files and folders/system state should be selected in the Azure Backup agent interface (see Figure 5-18).

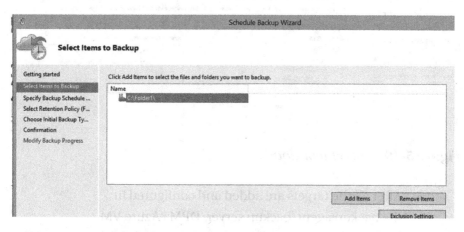

Figure 5-18. *Target file and folder selection*

14. For Azure Backup server and DPM, the initial configuration involves the installation of a DPM agent on the target server. Afterward, a protection group should be created for the workloads. The Azure Backup server/DPM automatically detects the workloads for backup. If the machine has Exchange installed, for example, the Exchange mailbox databases are automatically detected by the backup wizard when creating the protection group (see Figure 5-19).

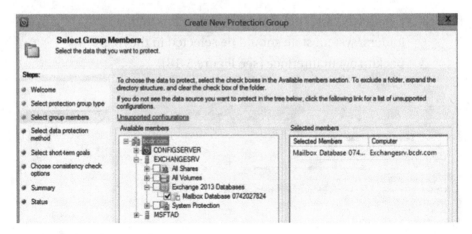

Figure 5-19. *Target workload*

15. After all the targets are added and configured in the backup agent/backup server/DPM/ Azure VM backup, the status can be reviewed directly from the Azure portal. Go to Recovery Services vault ➤ Protected Items ➤ Backup Items (see Figure 5-20).

Figure 5-20. *Listed of backup items in the portal*

Azure Site Recovery for IaaS (Preview)

Azure Backup does scheduled backup of VMs at specified time intervals to address the data and application resiliency concerns of environments hosted in Azure. If you have stringent recovery time objectives (RTOs) and recovery point objectives (RPOs) defined in a *business continuity and disaster recovery* (BCDR) strategy, Azure Site Recovery (ASR) could be the better choice because it replicates data continuously to a different region in Azure. Note that this service is in preview at the time of writing this book. It is recommended to include ASR in the architecture to enable environment-level resiliency once the service becomes generally available. ASR for Azure VMs can be enabled directly from the Azure portal with minimal configuration steps.

While Azure Backup requires the vault be in the same region as IaaS VMs, ASR mandates that to enable replication of IaaS VMs, the vault should be in a different region. This helps ensure the availability of the vault in the event of a disaster affecting Azure datacenters in a specific region.

1. To start ASR configuration for an Azure VM, open the **Recovery Services vault ➤ Get started ➤ Site Recovery ➤ Step1: Replicate Application**. Select the source, location, and resource group (see Figure 5-21).

Figure 5-21. *Select source settings*

2. Select the VM to be replicated (see Figure 5-22).

Figure 5-22. *Select VM*

3. Select the target region from the drop-down menu
    (see Figure 5-23).

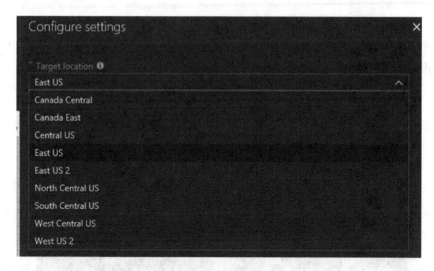

Figure 5-23. *Select target region*

4. Select the target resource group, network, and
    storage if required. By default, new storage accounts
    and networks are created for the replicated VMs,
    but you can customize these settings to select the
    storage and the network of your choice
    (see Figure 5-24).

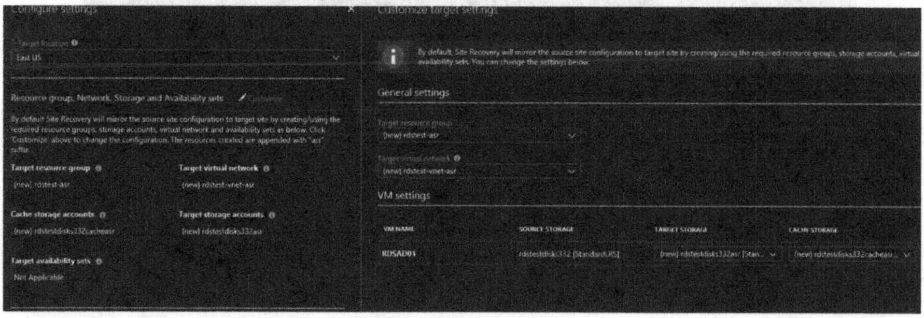

Figure 5-24. *Configure target settings*

The cache storage is also required in this architecture at the source location. Cache storage is used for temporarily storing VM changes before sending them over to the destination storage.

5. You can also customize the replication policy settings to change the number of hours for which the recovery point should be retained, or the number of app-consistent snapshots to be taken in an hour (see Figure 5-25).

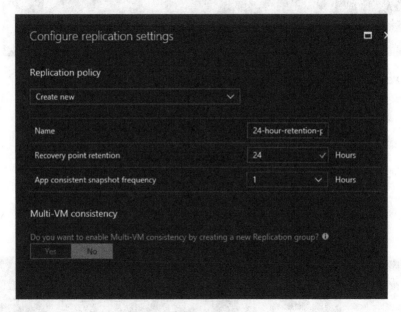

Figure 5-25. *Replication policy configuration*

6. If you want to replicate and failover multiple VMs,
    select the option to create a replication group
    and select the VMs that are part of the replication
    group. This replication could impact workload
    performance and should be opted only when a
    multi-VM consistent snapshot is a requirement
    (see Figure 5-26).

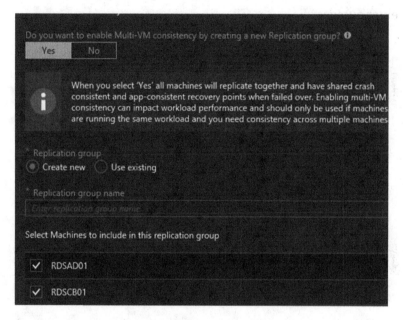

Figure 5-26. *Multi-VM replication*

In the subsequent steps, the target resources are created and
replication is enabled. Once the replication is completed, the VM is listed
at **Recovery Services vault ➤ Protected items ➤ Replicated items**. From
this interface, you can initiate a test failover or planned failovers for the VM
to the Azure destination region and resource group. This ensures VM and
application resiliency against Azure datacenter region failures.

Summary

This chapter discussed the different considerations and options available to build resiliency in an Azure infrastructure. For storage level resiliency, Azure managed disks in conjunction with availability sets should be considered. Compute resiliency can be attained through either availability sets or availability zones. Azure Backup and site recovery solutions should also be included in the mix to ensure resiliency against data loss and datacenter outages.

CHAPTER 6

Design for High Availability in Azure

Infrastructure is the backbone of services offered by organizations. Designing environments for high availability from the ground up to avoid single point of failures is particularly important. The end goal is to ensure minimal interruption to the user in the event of a platform, VM, or service failure. When the infrastructure is hosted in Microsoft Azure, the design should leverage platform-level features and services whenever possible, and use third-party tools if applicable. This chapter focuses on the features and services that should be included in any Azure IaaS architecture for highly available environments.

Availability Sets

Availability sets take care of underlying Azure platform availability in planned maintenance or unplanned outages. Microsoft Azure offers a 99.95% SLA if more than one VM is deployed in an availability set. Availability sets and load balancers are recommended design best practices to ensure platform and application availability. Availability sets take care of platform-level disruptions, but they do not protect against OS or application level issues that could affect the availability of hosted workloads.

© Shijimol Ambi Karthikeyan 2018
S. Ambi Karthikeyan, *Practical Microsoft Azure IaaS*,
https://doi.org/10.1007/978-1-4842-3763-2_6

Fault Domains and Update Domains

VMs are automatically distributed across fault domains, and they update domains in an availability set. A fault domain is a single point of failure in terms of physical rack, power, networking, and so forth. In a scenario where there are two VMs in an availability set with two fault domains, they are placed in fault domain 0 and fault domain 1, respectively. If a third VM is added to the availability set, it is automatically placed in fault domain 0. Please note that this placement is not user configurable except for the number of fault domains. If the event of a maintenance/downtime, even if the rack representing fault domain 0 is down, the application is available from the VMs in fault domain 1 (see Figure 6-1).

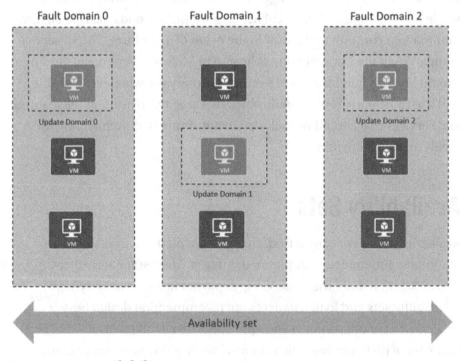

Figure 6-1. *Availability set*

Update domains become relevant when a VM must be rebooted to complete maintenance activities. When distributed across update domains, the VMs are protected from simultaneous reboots. The Azure platform ensures that only VMs in a single update domain in an availability set is rebooted at any given time during maintenance. There is a 30 minutes gap provided for the VMs to get back online before the VMs in the next update domain are rebooted. If there are three update domains, the first three VMs in an availability set are placed in update domain 0, 1, and 2, and the fourth VM is placed sequentially back in update domain 0.

Availability Set Configuration

Availability sets can be configured from the **Configure optional features** settings when creating a new VM (see Figure 6-2).

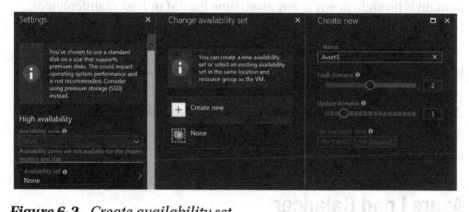

Figure 6-2. *Create availability set*

By default, availability sets are created with two fault domains and five update domains. The number of fault domains can be increased to 20. There can be either two or three fault domains, depending on the region selected.

VMs should be added to an availability set when they are created. To add a VM to an existing availability set or to change the availability set of a VM, the VM should be deleted and re-created.

Load Balancing Client Requests

Service disruptions can be caused by platform, OS, or application issues. Infrastructure design should ensure a seamless user experience. While availability sets takes care of platform-related downtime and maintenance, application availability could still be affected; for example, only one update domain is brought down at any given time for VM or host maintenance. However, if the user tries to access the application when the VM is down, it is presented as a service disruption from a user perspective. It is important to redirect users to the VMs in the available update domains in such scenarios. Load Balancer, Application Manager, and Traffic Manager are the three different options available in Azure to achieve this. They also distribute traffic to a back-end pool of machines to ensure that the load is evenly distributed.

Azure Load Balancer

Azure Load Balancer works at Layer 4 (transport layer, TCP/UDP). It distributes incoming traffic in internal networks and from the Internet. The former is called an *internal load balancer* and latter is called a *public load balancer*. Load balancers can also redirect traffic to a specific port on one of the back-end VMs.

Traffic reaching the front-end IP of the load balancer is distributed evenly to the back-end pool of VMs using a five-tuple hash-based algorithm defined in the *load balancer rule*. The load balancer rule consists of the source IP, source port, destination IP, destination port, and IP protocol.

There are two types of distribution modes in a load balancer: hash-based and source IP affinity mode. In hash-based distribution mode, traffic is distributed to a back-end VM based on the five-tuple hash rule, and the traffic from one source is sent to the same back-end VM in a single transport session. If the client starts a new session with a new source port, the traffic could be redirected to a different back-end VM (see Figure 6-3).

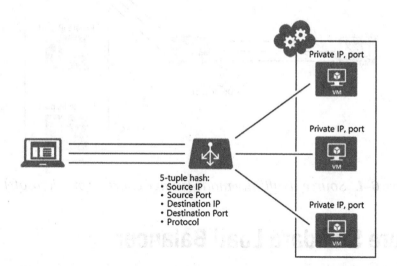

Figure 6-3. *Five-tuple hash-based algorithm (image courtesy of Microsoft)*

If you want to configure a load balancer to send to the same back-end VM, throughout the session, the source IP affinity mode should be used. In source IP affinity mode, either a two-tuple or a three-tuple algorithm is used to map traffic to one of the back-end VMs throughout the session. Source IP affinity mode is used in specific use cases and scenarios like a remote desktop gateway, media uploads, and so forth (see Figure 6-4).

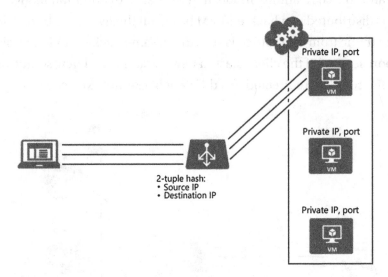

Figure 6-4. *Source IP affinity mode (image courtesy of Microsoft)*

Azure Standard Load Balancer

The Azure Standard Load Balancer is a new SKU that caters to enterprise workloads. It provides more scalability than the basic SKU load balancer. It is recommended to use the Standard Load Balancer for all new design scenarios because of the following reasons.

- Standard load balancers can support up to 1000 instances in the back-end pool.

- Basic load balancers can be configured only for VMs in an availability set or as part of VM scale sets. Standard load balancers may have VMs that are not part of availability sets in the back-end pool or are from different availability sets.

- Standard load balancers support availability zones and allow for the configuration of zone-redundant and zonal front ends, and zone redundant protection for outbound traffic flow.

- High availability ports available in standard load balancers allow all traffic that reaches the load balancer at any port to be forwarded to the back-end VM pool. This is especially useful in architectures using network virtual appliances (NVA); for example, it can be used to meet specific security requirements where all the traffic reaching a load balancer should be distributed to a back-end pool having x number of NVAs for high availability purposes.

- Azure Standard Load Balancer has a 99.99% SLA associated with it, whereas there are no specific SLAs tied to a basic load balancer.

Azure Application Gateway

The Azure Application Gateway works as a load balancer at Layer 7. Unlike the Layer 4 load balancer, the traffic flow is redirected based on the URL that is being accessed by the user. It is more suitable for use cases where there are multiple sites in multiple back-end pools, and the incoming traffic needs to be mapped to a single public IP/DNS entry (see Figure 6-5).

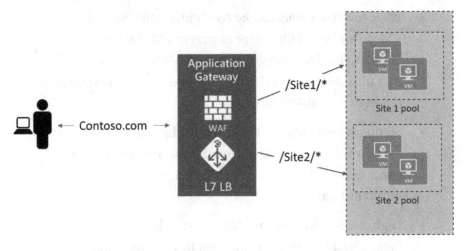

Figure 6-5. *Azure Application Gateway*

The Azure Application Gateway provides advanced routing and load balancing capabilities based on access URL patterns. In the example shown in Figure 6-5, the traffic is sent to the site 1 back-end pool if the user accesses Contoso.com/site1, and to the site 2 back-end pool if the URL contains Contoso.com/site2.

The following are some other features.

- Supports HTTP to HTTPS redirection for secure application access.

- Multiple sites can be hosted behind the same application gateway by separating them across multiple server pools.

- In addition to load balancing HTTP/ HTTPS traffic, Azure Application Gateway has additional capabilities built in, such as SSL offloading, cookie-based session affinity, and web application firewalls.

Azure Traffic Manager

Azure Traffic Manager uses DNS-based load balancing to distribute traffic to multiple endpoints in the back end. These endpoints could be VMs in Azure with public IPs, Azure web apps, cloud services, or they could even be on-premise endpoints. It is most significant in hybrid cloud use cases, where, for example, one instance of the application is hosted in the cloud and another instance is hosted on-premise.

It improves the availability of important applications by monitoring your Azure services or external websites and services, and it automatically directs your customers to a new location when there is a failure (see Figure 6-6).

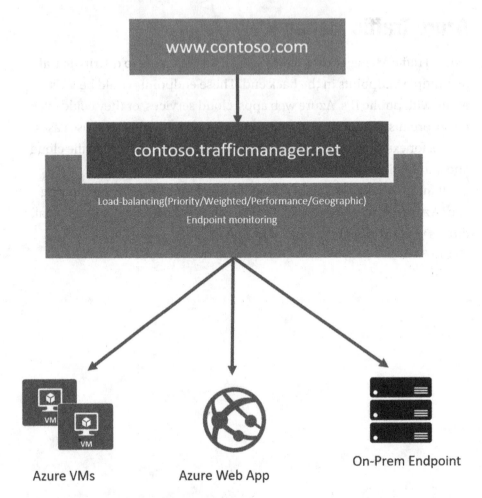

Figure 6-6. *Azure Traffic Manager*

There are four types of routing mechanisms available in Azure Load Balancer: priority, weighted, performance, and geographic. Depending on the configured routing mechanism, the traffic manager returns a DNS entry of one of the back-end endpoints as a response to the user request. This DNS entry is then used to access the endpoint directly. It is important to do that. Unlike Azure Load Balancer and Azure Application Gateway, Azure Traffic Manager is not involved in any actual traffic routing or package forwarding to back-end endpoints. Instead, it returns the DNS entry of endpoints so that users can directly access them.

Let's briefly explore the routing methods that can be configured in Traffic Manager.

- **Priority traffic-routing**. This is helpful in implementing primary-secondary logic among the back-end endpoints. The endpoint designated as primary is always the first priority. If that endpoint is not available, the traffic is sent to the endpoint designated as secondary. A third endpoint can be added, and traffic is forwarded to this endpoint if both the primary and secondary are not available.

- **Weighted traffic-routing**. In this routing mechanism, weights are assigned to all endpoints, and the traffic is distributed based on the value of the weights. Weight can be any integer between 1 and 1000. The endpoints with highest visit are returned more frequently, resulting in more traffic to the endpoint. If the traffic is to be evenly distributed, assign the same weight to all endpoints.

- **Performance traffic-routing**. The endpoint that is hosted in the datacenter with the lowest latency to the source IP is returned to the requestor, thereby ensuring a better user experience.

- **Geographic traffic-routing**. In this routing mechanism, each endpoint has a geographic region associated with it. When a request reaches the traffic manager from any of those geographic regions, the endpoints mapped to those specific regions are returned. This helps in meeting compliance requirements when users from different geographic regions access applications hosted in multiple Azure datacenter regions.

Design Hybrid Connections for HA

On-premise connectivity can be achieved through a VPN or ExpressRoute. ExpressRoute is SLA-backed with assured availability from Microsoft and has redundancy built into the solution. It is the recommended solution to extend your datacenter to Azure. However, ExpressRoute is more costly than VPNs, and so many small and medium-sized businesses opt for VPN connections. The Azure VPN gateway consists of two instances in an active-standby configuration by default. However, there could be a brief disruption when the standby instance takes over the connection during a disruption. To avoid this, additional redundancy can be built into the VPN configuration.

Active-Active VPN Configuration

Instead of the default active-passive settings, the Azure VPN gateway can be configured in active-active mode. Two Azure VPN gateways are simultaneously connected to the on-prem gateway, and traffic flows through both the connections. In the event of a disruption in one of the gateways, the other gateway remains active, and traffic is switched over simultaneously to this active channel (see Figure 6-7).

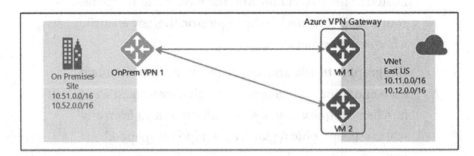

Figure 6-7. *Active-active VPN*

Active-Active Dual Redundancy

In the configuration shown in Figure 6-7, the on-prem gateway represents a single point of failure. You can improve availability by adding an active gateway at the on-premise end, resulting in full-mesh connectivity (see Figure 6-8).

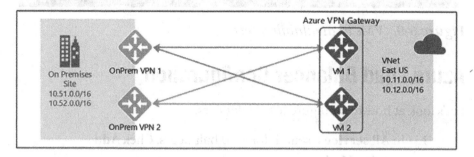

Figure 6-8. *Active-active full-mesh*

There are four IPsec tunnels in this architecture. Traffic is distributed across the tunnels, resulting in better throughput. BGP (border gateway protocol) is required to enable this active-active connection to two on-premise gateways.

Sample Use Case and Implementation

Let's explore a sample use case of implementing high availability using a load balancer and availability sets for the web tier of an application. Note that the web VMs to be load balanced were already created and added to the availability set as a prerequisite (see Figure 6-9).

Figure 6-9. *VMs in availability sets*

Azure Load Balancer Configuration

Let's look at how to configure load balancers.

1. In **All services**, search for load balancers. Click **Add new load balancer**.

2. Provide mandatory inputs such as the type of load balancer (Internal/Public), load balancer SKU, public IP, resource group, and region (see Figure 6-10).

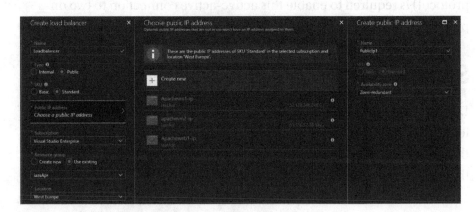

Figure 6-10. *Load balancer configuration*

Note If you select the standard SKU, the associated public is automatically from the standard SKU. The public IP can be configured as zone-redundant for additional resiliency.

---

3. Once the load balancer is created, click **Settings**. The public IP address is created and attached to the load balancer and is listed under **Frontend IP configuration**. You can add more public IP addresses to the load balancer if needed. The default limit for standard load balancer is ten for basic and standard load balancers (see Figure 6-11).

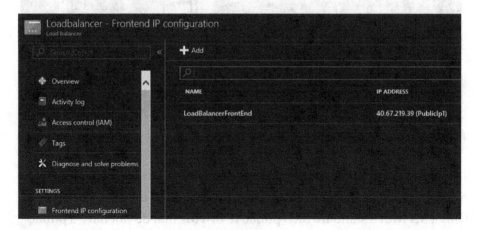

Figure 6-11. *Front-end IP configuration*

4. Configure the back-end pool from Settings ➤
    Backend pools (see Figure 6-12).

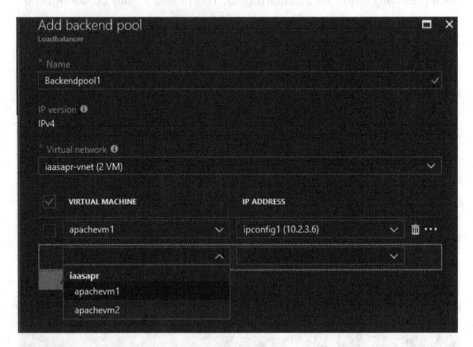

Figure 6-12. *Create the back-end pool*

Since we are using a standard load balancer, there are certain
restrictions in the virtual networks that can be added to the back-end pool.
Only VMs with a standard SKU public IP or VMs that do not have a public
IP attached can be added to the back-end pool of a standard load balancer.
To load balance across VMs connected to a different network, another
back-end pool should be added.

Load balancers use health probes to constantly check the services in the back-end pool of machines that are up and running. Health probes can be configured from **Settings ➤ Health probes**. This endpoint can either be an HTTP path or a service running at a TCP port. By default, the load balancer checks the endpoint every five seconds, and it is deemed unhealthy if it does not respond after two consecutive checks (see Figure 6-13).

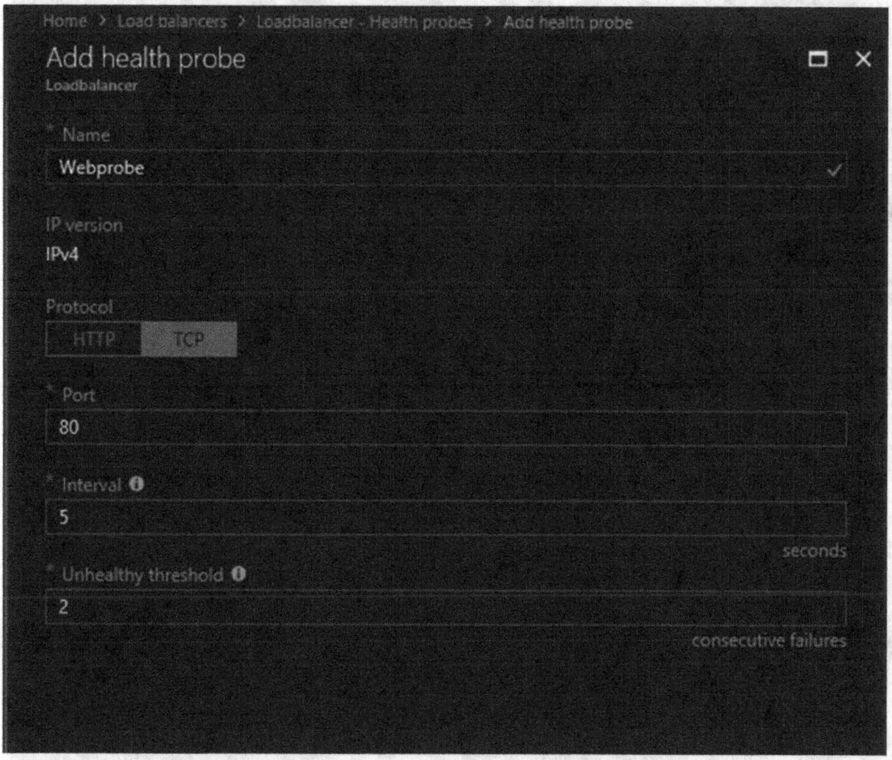

Figure 6-13. Health probe

5.   Create a load balancer rule using the front-end IP,
     back-end pool, and health probes (see Figure 6-14).

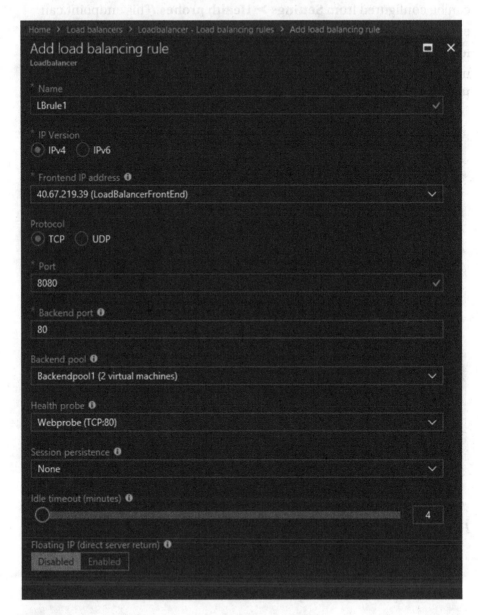

Figure 6-14. Configure load balancing rules

In this example, the rule is configured to accept traffic at port 8080 and sends the traffic to port 80 in the VMs in the back-end pool. The health probe checks every five seconds if the service is running at port 80 in all VMs in the pool, and it sends traffic only to the healthy nodes. Session persistence can also be configured for the client IP or client IP and protocol if required. The option of floating IP should be used only when configuring SQL Always On availability group.

6. Instead of load balancing the traffic across multiple VMs, if you want to redirect traffic to a port of a specific VM in the back-end pool, create an inbound NAT rule from Settings ➤ Inbound NAT rules (see Figure 6-15).

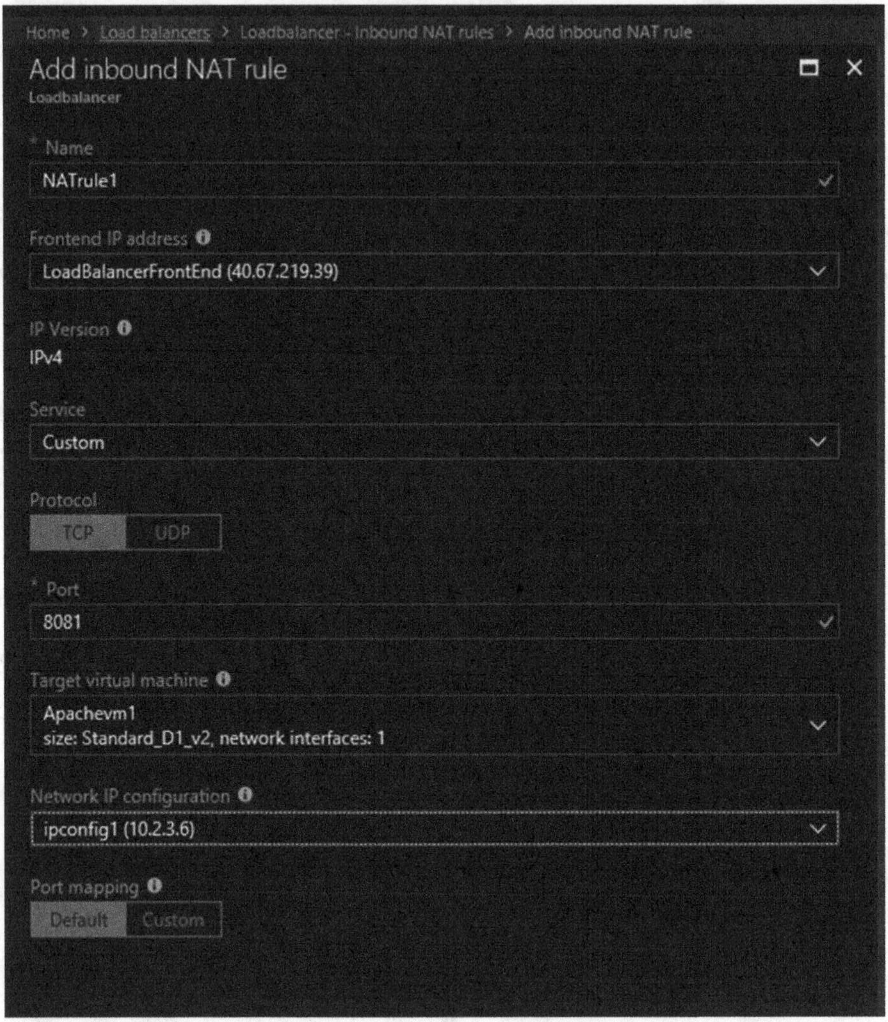

Figure 6-15.   Inbound NAT rule

In Figure 6-15, the traffic received by the load balancer at port 8081 is redirected to port 8081 on of one of the VMs.

In this use case, the VMs do not have a public IP configured, and hence, Internet traffic does not reach them directly. This is in accordance with Azure security best practices. The VM has an inbound rule configured

in a network security group (NSG) that allows inbound traffic at port 80
to access the hosted VM, and the traffic reaches the VM only via the load
balancer (see Figure 6-16).

Figure 6-16. *VM NSG rule*

Note that in the rule, the service tag is selected as Internet and not Azure Load Balancer, even though the traffic reaches the VM only through a load balancer. This is because Azure Load Balancer routes traffic from the Internet to the VMs without any change to the incoming package. Hence, the configuration will not work if you select Azure Load Balancer instead of the Internet.

If the entire configuration is done correctly, the website page is accessible at `http://<frontend IP of load balancer>:8080`.

Azure Application Gateway Configuration

The following is the process for configuring Azure Application Gateway.

1. Create a standard application gateway in the standard tier.

2. Select the SKU size (medium or high, the recommended starting SKUs for production workloads). The instance count can be kept at default (i.e., 2, which is recommended for production workloads) (see Figure 6-17).

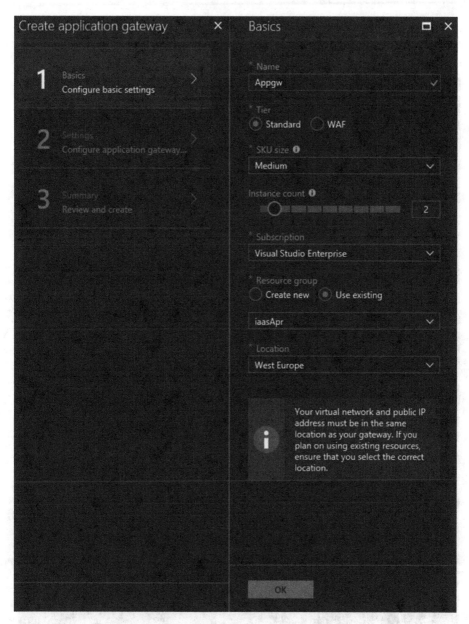

Figure 6-17. *Create Application Gateway*

3. Select **Configure the application gateway settings**
    (see Figure 6-18).

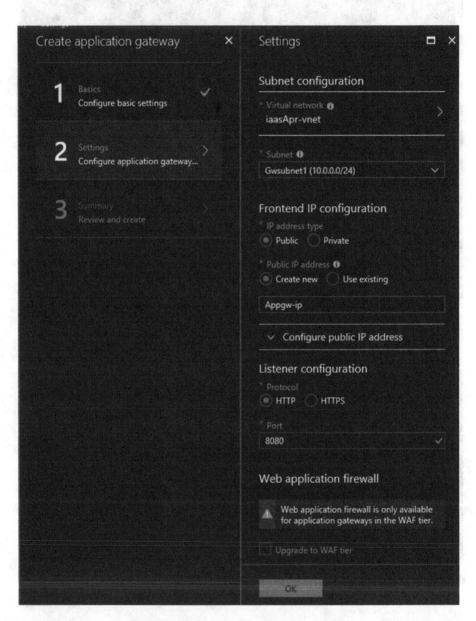

Figure 6-18. *Configure application gateway settings*

Application gateways should be created in the same VNet to which the VMs are connected. However, be mindful that the application gateway should be created in a subnet in the VNet that do not have any other resources connected to it. An application gateway needs a public IP in the basic SKU and an HTTP or HTTPs endpoint with the target port.

4. In this use case, we use port 8080, as it was configured for the load balancer. Review and click **OK** to create the application gateway.

5. Click Settings ➤ Backend pools. Select the default back-end pool and add targets, or create a new back-end pool (see Figure 6-19).

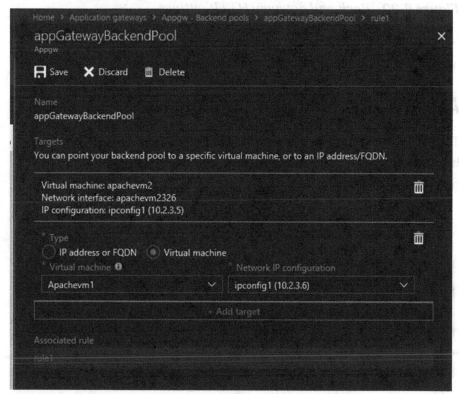

Figure 6-19. *Create application gateway back-end pool*

6. Click the associated rule. Configure the back-end
    HTTP settings if you wish to change the default port
    settings (see Figure 6-20).

Figure 6-20. *Back-end gateway HTTP settings*

Once configured correctly, the application is available at
`http://<Public IP of application Gateway>:8080`

Azure Traffic Manager Configuration

To get this use case to work with Azure Traffic Manager, the VMs should
have an associated public IP. In addition, the public IP should have a DNS
name associated with it.

1. Go to Public IP addresses ➤ IP of the VM ➤
    Configuration (see Figure 6-21).

Figure 6-21. *IP address DNS configuration*

2. Once the public IPs and DNS names are configured, they can be added to the back-end pool of Azure Traffic Manager. Select the Traffic Manager profile and then **Settings ➤ Endpoints** (see Figure 6-22).

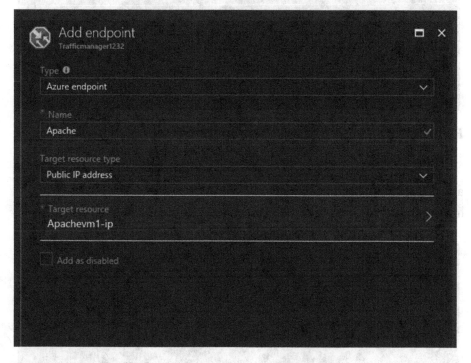

Figure 6-22. *Traffic manager endpoint configuration*

- Select **Azure endpoint** as the endpoint type.

- Provide a suitable name for each endpoint.

- Select **Public IP address** as the target resource type. Select the IP from the listed public IP addresses.

3. Configure the endpoint monitoring to check for endpoint health at a defined port. Fast endpoint failover settings decide how fast a back-end endpoint is deemed unhealthy and users are redirected away from it (see Figure 6-23).

Figure 6-23. *Traffic manager endpoint monitoring*

If the service is up and running, the endpoints are listed as enabled and online in the traffic manager overview. The website is accessible at `http://<Traffic manager DNS name>` (see Figure 6-24).

Figure 6-24. *Endpoints listed in Azure Traffic Manager*

Summary

Building high availability in Azure applications needs careful consideration of factors at the platform, network, and application layers. Although availability sets ensure platform-level availability, they should be combined with tools like Azure Load Balancer, Azure Application Gateway, and Azure Traffic Manager to ensure application availability.

CHAPTER 7

Automated Provisioning and Performance Fine-Tuning

For a large-scale infrastructure deployment, whether in Azure or on-premise, it is important to automate as many tasks as possible to reduce human effort and error. Ongoing monitoring and performance fine-tuning are also important operational aspects of an Azure IaaS deployment. When carefully planned and managed, these factors ensure optimal utilization of resources and maximize ROI. This chapter focuses on the tools available in Azure for automated provisioning, monitoring, and performance fine-tuning.

Azure ARM Template Deployment

Azure Resource Manager (ARM) templates were introduced in the Azure Resource Manager model to facilitate the automation of repeated deployments and to ensure consistency across environments.

© Shijimol Ambi Karthikeyan 2018
S. Ambi Karthikeyan, *Practical Microsoft Azure IaaS*,
https://doi.org/10.1007/978-1-4842-3763-2_7

The ARM template is basically a JSON file that defines an Azure environment and its components and dependencies. Other than Azure IaaS resources, the connected PaaS resources—such as SQL Database, App Service, and so forth—can also be defined in an ARM template. Once defined and deployed, the same template can be used to rebuild the environment at any time. VM names, database names, and so forth, can change across deployments, and they can be defined as parameters in the ARM template.

You can also create separate templates for different application tiers and link them to a main template. This provides granularity in terms of template management, and enables recycle and reuse to cater to diverse use cases.

Let's explore the basic constructs of an ARM template.

```
{
    "$schema": "http://schema.management.azure.com/
    schemas/2015-01-01/deploymentTemplate.json#",
    "contentVersion": "",
    "parameters": {  },
    "variables": {  },
    "resources": [  ],
    "outputs": {  }
}
```

$schema, contentVersion, and resources are the mandatory elements in an ARM template, whereas parameters, variables, and outputs are optional components.

- $schema defines the location of the JSON schema, and the value should be same as what is shown in the code.

- contentVersion defines the components' version. This may be left blank or updated with the version relevant to specific deployments.

- `parameters` refers to values that could change across template deployments; for example, environment prefixes, resource group, VM name, and so forth.

- `variables` are JSON fragments that can be used anywhere inside an ARM template to create values such as the resource ID or resource name.

- `resources` defines the Azure components to be created or updated by ARM template.

- `outputs` is the result of the deployment.

Templates can be deployed in multiple ways from the Azure portal.

1. Search for templates from **All services** (see Figure 7-1).

Figure 7-1. *Search for templates in All services*

2. Click **Add**, and then provide the name and description (see Figure 7-2).

Figure 7-2. *Name and description of template*

3. Click **Add template**. Edit the contents of the
    template and click OK. Here we start with the
    default template content and edit it later
    (see Figure 7-3).

Figure 7-3. *Template content*

4. Select the template and click Edit ➤ ARM template
    to make changes to the template.

The following sample template creates a VM and adds it
to an existing subnet.

```
{
    "$schema": "https://schema.management.azure.com/
    schemas/2015-01-01/deploymentTemplate.json#",
    "contentVersion": "1.0.0.0",
    "parameters": {
        "adminUsername": {
            "type": "String",
            "metadata": {
                "description": "Username for the Virtual Machine."
            }
        },
        "adminPassword": {
            "type": "SecureString",
            "metadata": {
```

```
            "description": "Password for the Virtual Machine."
        }
    },
    "dnsLabelPrefix": {
        "type": "String",
        "metadata": {
            "description": "Unique DNS Name for the Public
            IP used to access the Virtual Machine."
        }
    },
    "windowsOSVersion": {
        "defaultValue": "2016-Datacenter",
        "allowedValues": [
            "2008-R2-SP1",
            "2012-Datacenter",
            "2012-R2-Datacenter",
            "2016-Nano-Server",
            "2016-Datacenter-with-Containers",
            "2016-Datacenter"
        ],
        "type": "String",
        "metadata": {
            "description": "The Windows version for the
            VM. This will pick a fully patched image of
            this given Windows version."
        }
    }
},
"variables": {
    "storageAccountName": "[concat(uniquestring(resource
    Group().id), 'sawinvm')]",
```

```
    "nicName": "myVMNic",
    "addressPrefix": "172.16.0.0/16",
    "subnetName": "db",
    "subnetPrefix": "172.16.0.0/24",
    "publicIPAddressName": "myPublicIP",
    "vmName": "WinVMdb01",
    "virtualNetworkName": "vnet01",
    "subnetRef": "[resourceId('Microsoft.Network/
    virtualNetworks/subnets', variables('virtualNetworkName'),
    variables('subnetName'))]"
},
"resources": [
    {
        "type": "Microsoft.Storage/storageAccounts",
        "sku": {
            "name": "Standard_LRS"
        },
        "kind": "Storage",
        "name": "[variables('storageAccountName')]",
        "apiVersion": "2016-01-01",
        "location": "[resourceGroup().location]",
        "properties": {}
    },
    {
        "type": "Microsoft.Network/publicIPAddresses",
        "name": "[variables('publicIPAddressName')]",
        "apiVersion": "2016-03-30",
        "location": "[resourceGroup().location]",
        "properties": {
            "publicIPAllocationMethod": "Dynamic",
            "dnsSettings": {
```

```
            "domainNameLabel": "[parameters('dnsLabel
            Prefix')]"
        }
    }
},
{

    "type": "Microsoft.Network/networkInterfaces",
    "name": "[variables('nicName')]",
    "apiVersion": "2016-03-30",
    "location": "[resourceGroup().location]",
    "properties": {
        "ipConfigurations": [
            {
                "name": "ipconfig1",
                "properties": {
                    "privateIPAllocationMethod": "Dynamic",
                    "publicIPAddress": {
                        "id": "[resourceId('Microsoft.
                        Network/publicIPAddresses',
                        variables('publicIPAddress
                        Name'))]"
                    },
                    "subnet": {
                        "id": "[variables('subnetRef')]"
                    }
                }
            }
        ]
    },
    "dependsOn": [
```

```
            "[resourceId('Microsoft.Network/
            publicIPAddresses/', variables
            ('publicIPAddressName'))]"
        ]
    },
    {
        "type": "Microsoft.Compute/virtualMachines",
        "name": "[variables('vmName')]",
        "apiVersion": "2017-03-30",
        "location": "[resourceGroup().location]",
        "properties": {
            "hardwareProfile": {
                "vmSize": "Standard_A2"
            },
            "osProfile": {
                "computerName": "[variables('vmName')]",
                "adminUsername": "[parameters
                ('adminUsername')]",
                "adminPassword": "[parameters('adminPassword')]"
            },
            "storageProfile": {
                "imageReference": {
                    "publisher": "MicrosoftWindowsServer",
                    "offer": "WindowsServer",
                    "sku": "[parameters('windowsOSVersion')]",
                    "version": "latest"
                },
                "osDisk": {
                    "createOption": "FromImage"
                },
                "dataDisks": [
```

```json
                    {
                        "diskSizeGB": 1023,
                        "lun": 0,
                        "createOption": "Empty"
                    }
                ]
            },
            "networkProfile": {
                "networkInterfaces": [
                    {
                        "id": "[resourceId('Microsoft.
                        Network/networkInterfaces',
                        variables('nicName'))]"
                    }
                ]
            },
            "diagnosticsProfile": {
                "bootDiagnostics": {
                    "enabled": true,
                    "storageUri": "[reference(resourceId
                    ('Microsoft.Storage/storageAccounts/',
                    variables('storageAccountName'))).
                    primaryEndpoints.blob]"
                }
            }
        },
        "dependsOn": [
            "[resourceId('Microsoft.Storage/storageAccounts/',
            variables('storageAccountName'))]",
            "[resourceId('Microsoft.Network/
            networkInterfaces/', variables('nicName'))]"
```

```
            ]
        }
    ],
    "outputs": {
        "hostname": {
            "type": "String",
            "value": "[reference(variables('publicIPAddress
            Name')).dnsSettings.fqdn]"
        }
    }
}
```

Let's explore the different components of this template.

- The parameters defined here are the VM
  username/password, the DNS name of the public
  IP, and the VM operating system.

- The VM network and storage details are listed
  under variables. The VM name is also listed as a
  variable. Depending on the use case, you might
  want to convert that to a parameter so that the
  value can be changed across deployment.

- The components listed under the resources section
  is created when the template is deployed.

- All the required components for the VM—such as
  storage accounts, public IP address, and network
  interface—are created before proceeding to the VM
  machine creation, because these components are
  referenced during the VM deployment.

5. Click **Deploy** to start the template deployment
    (see Figure 7-4).

Figure 7-4. *Deploy template*

6. When you deploy a template, you must select either
    an existing resource group or a new resource group.
    The values of mandatory parameters should also be
    provided under Settings. Click **Purchase** to start the
    VM deployment (see Figure 7-5).

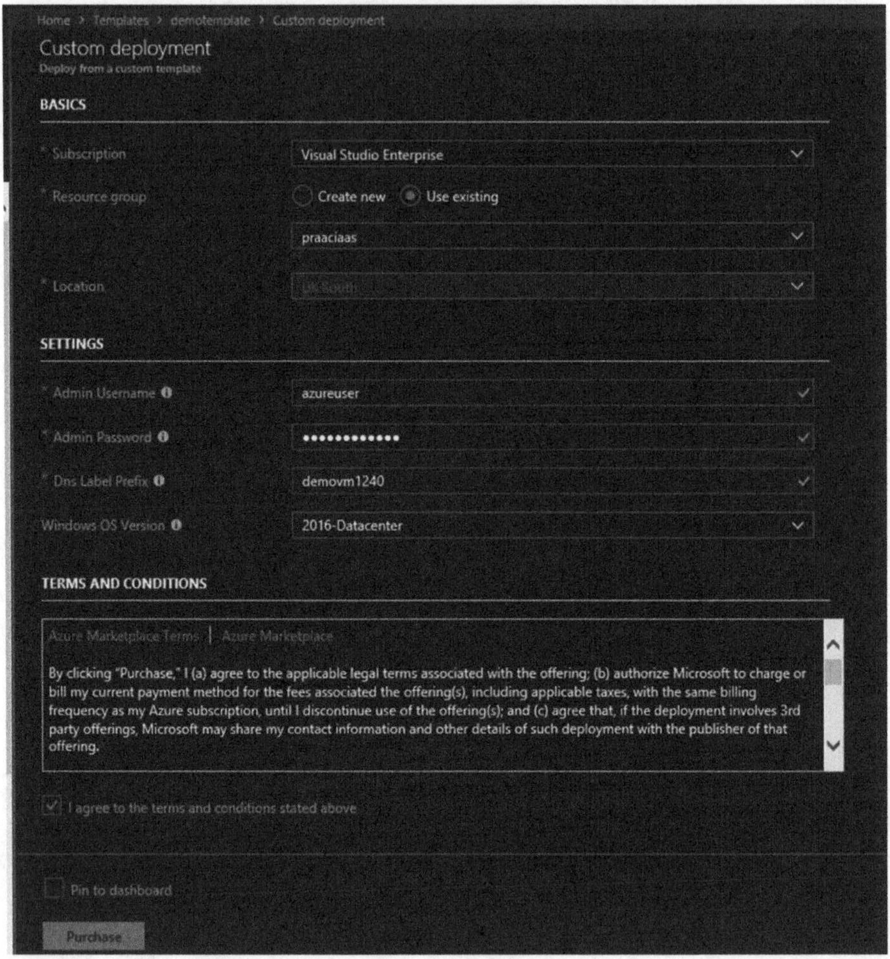

Figure 7-5. *Template parameters*

You can review the status of the deployment to make sure that the resources were created successfully. The Resource section components are listed in the status output of the template deployment (see Figure 7-6).

Figure 7-6. *Deployment status*

Note You can also deploy the template directly from the Azure Quickstart templates gallery hosted on GitHub at `https://azure.microsoft.com/en-in/resources/templates/`.

---

7.   Search for templates related to your use case; for
     example, SharePoint deployment (see Figure 7-7).

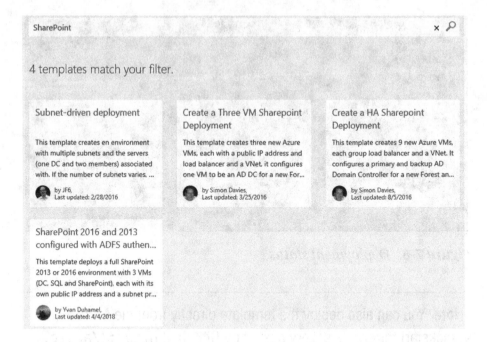

Figure 7-7. Search for templates

8. In addition to the ones created by Microsoft, these
    templates also include community-contributed
    ones. Select the template that you want to deploy
    to see more information about it, including the
    required parameters and the commands to deploy
    it using PowerShell/CLI. Alternatively, you can click
    Deploy to Azure to deploy the template to the Azure
    subscription that you are currently logged in to (see
    Figure 7-8).

Figure 7-8. *Select template*

9. Once you click **Deploy to Azure**, the deployment
    window opens and the input parameters are
    provided. The remaining steps are similar what was
    seen in the direct deployment from portal method.

You can also open GitHub templates directly from the Azure portal
by accessing the following URL after logging into your target Azure
subscription: `https://portal.azure.com/#create/Microsoft.Template`.

GitHub templates are listed. Select one to proceed with the
deployment (see Figure 7-9).

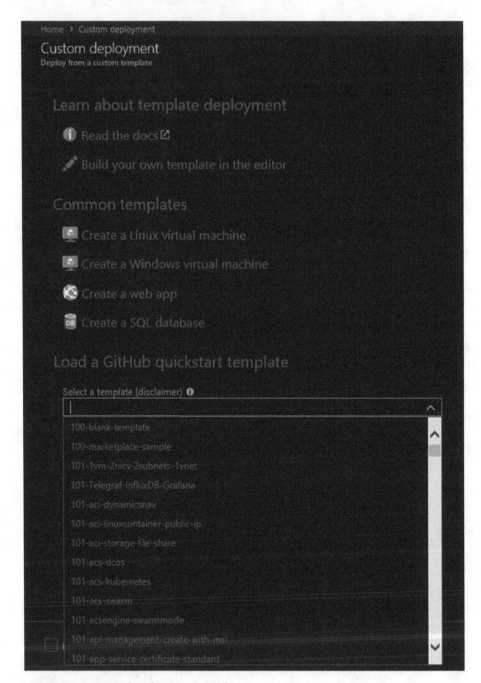

Figure 7-9. *Deploy from GitHub*

ARM Template: Infrastructure As Code Deployment

At a high level, infrastructure as code (IaC) is the way that you configure and manage your infrastructure, the same way that you would manage your application code. It leverages the concepts of continuous integration and deployment to update or provision your environment based on the changes made to the code. This section explores the setup and configuration of a continuous integration and continuous deployment (CI/CD) tool integrated with a source code repository for IaC deployment. The CI/CD tool used is VSTS and the source code repository is Git. The code is the ARM template JSON file and the related parameter files.

The following are the prerequisites:

- The Git repository to store the ARM templates and parameter files is created and cloned to the local machine.

- VSTS project is created.

- The Git repository is added to the VSTS project.

Configuration

Let's follow an approach for a build and deployment configuration that provides more control over the release process. The build process will produce an artifact whenever a change is made and committed to the ARM template. The release pipeline will leverage this artifact and deploy it to target environments, which in effect creates/updates the Azure environment.

Build Configuration

Let's start with the build configuration.

1. Create a new project and a build associated with it. Choose the **Empty process** option to start the build (see Figure 7-10).

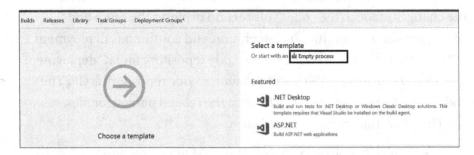

Figure 7-10. Build configuration

2. Enter the build's name and choose **Hosted** as the agent (see Figure 7-11).

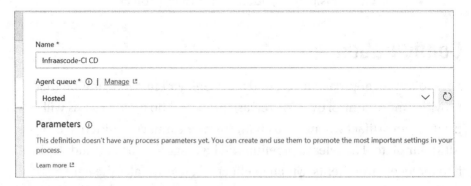

Figure 7-11. Build name

3. Add the tasks shown in Figure 7-12 from Tasks ➤ utility.

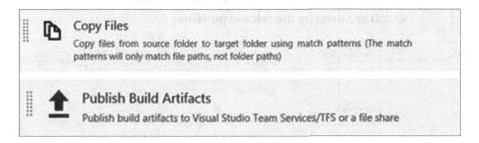

Figure 7-12. *Add tasks*

4. Configure the tasks in **Copy Files** (see Figure 7-13). In this step, the files from the build directory are copied to a staging directory. The build directory could contain all the relevant files required for deployment (for example, the ARM JSON and dependent files).

Copy Files ⓘ   ⏏ Link settings   ✕ Rem

Version 2.* ⌄

Display name *

Copy Files to: $(build.artifactstagingdirectory)

Source Folder ⓘ

$(agent.builddirectory)

Contents *   ⓘ

**

Target Folder *   ⓘ

$(build.artifactstagingdirectory)

Figure 7-13. *Copy files*

5.   Configure the **Publish Build Artifacts** task (see Figure 7-14). Here the contents of the staging directory are published as artifacts of the build, which are used by the release pipeline.

Figure 7-14. *Publish artifacts*

6.   Enable the trigger for continuous integration. Once the trigger is enabled in the project, the build starts as soon as a code commit is made to the repository (see Figure 7-15).

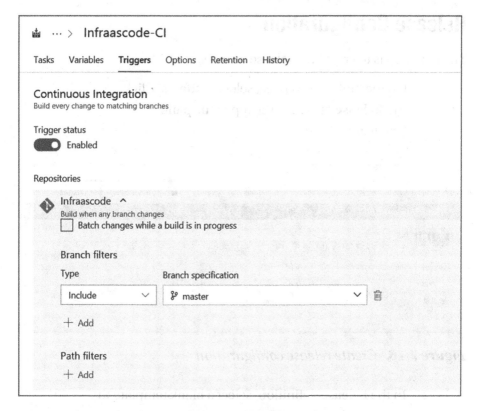

Figure 7-15. *Enable continuous integration*

The build configuration is completed and the required contents for deployment (i.e., the JSON file and the dependent files) are produced as artifacts of the build configuration. If you make any edits in the source files and commit them, the build will be triggered. On successful completion of the build, you can see the artifacts in VSTS.

Release Configuration

The next step is to create the release process.

1. On the build status page, select **Artifacts**. Click the **Release** option at the top of the pane (see Figure 7-16).

Figure 7-16. *Create release configuration*

2. In the Release definition, select a blank template to start with (see Figure 7-17).

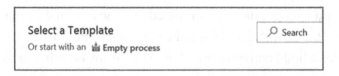

Figure 7-17. *Select blank template*

3. Provide the name of the first environment in the pipeline (see Figure 7-18).

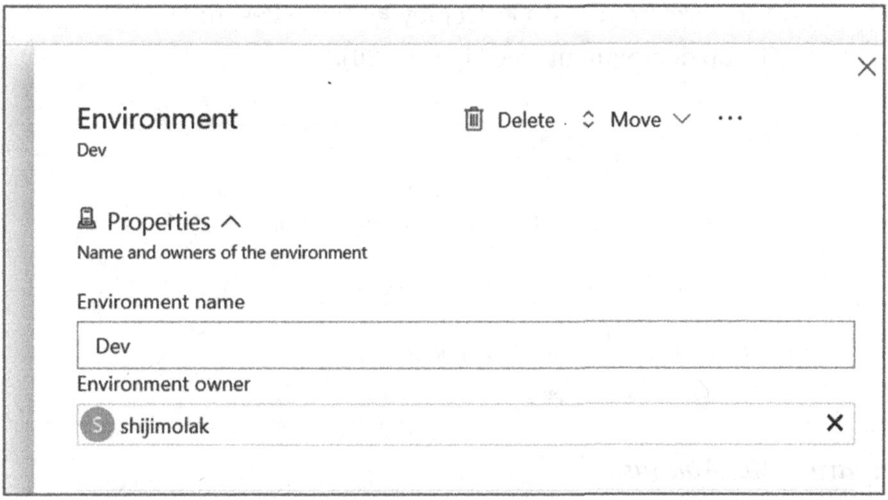

Environment
Dev

🗑 Delete   ⇕ Move ∨   ···   ✕

🖳 Properties ∧
Name and owners of the environment

Environment name

Dev

Environment owner

Ⓢ shijimolak   ✕

Figure 7-18. Environment name

4. The first environment is ready; it's time to add
    the tasks. Select the created environment
    (see Figure 7-19).

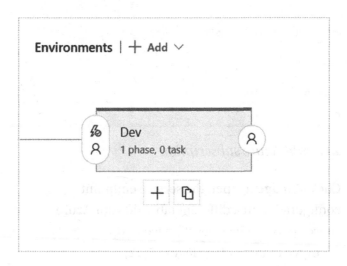

Figure 7-19. Select environment

5. Add tasks from Tasks ➤ Deploy ➤ Azure Resource
    Group deployment (see Figure 7-20).

Figure 7-20. Add task

6. Edit the settings of the added task and add your
    Azure subscription to VSTS as a service endpoint
    (see Figure 7-21).

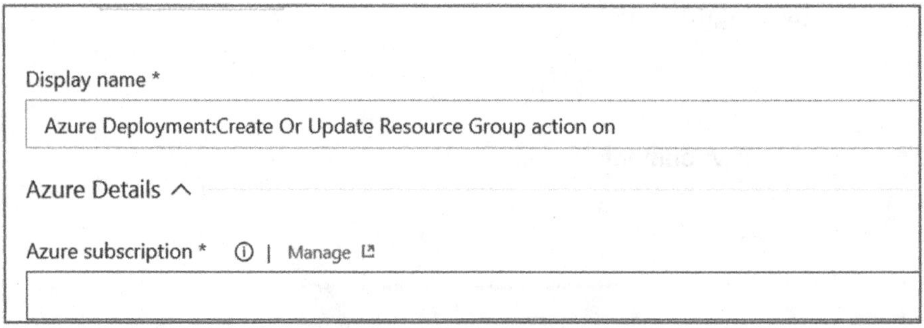

Figure 7-21. Add Azure subscription

7. Click **Manage** to open the service endpoint
    configuration in a different tab. Add your Azure
    subscription. Select New Service Endpoint ➤ Azure
    Resource Manager (see Figure 7-22).

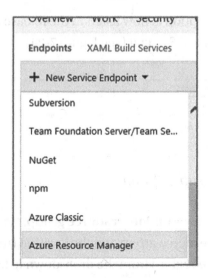

Figure 7-22. *Create new endpoint*

8. Add the subscription name. When you click OK, you are asked to log in to your Azure subscription to authenticate (see Figure 7-23).

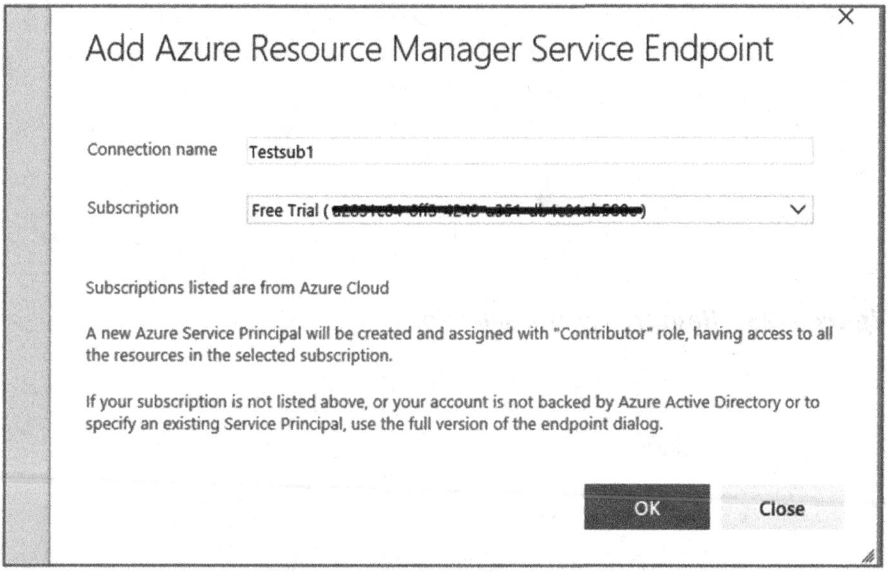

Figure 7-23. *Azure subscription login*

9. Your subscription is now listed in the release task drop-down list. Select it (see Figure 7-24).

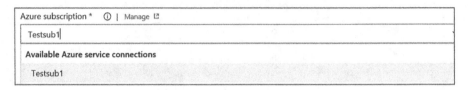

Figure 7-24. *Select subscription*

10. Select **Create or update resource group**. Choose the target resource group and the location (the target Azure region) from the drop-down list. The template location should be **Linked artifact** (see Figure 7-25).

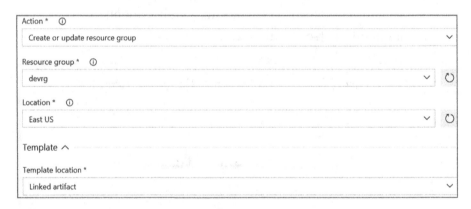

Figure 7-25. *Resource group selection*

11. Browse and select the ARM JSON file from the linked artifact (see Figure 7-26).

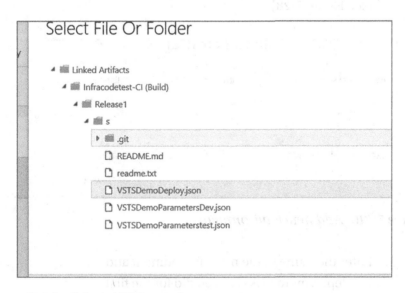

Figure 7-26. *Select ARM template*

12. Select the parameters JSON file parameters (depends on the target environment). Set the deployment mode to **Incremental** (see Figure 7-27).

Template *   ⓘ
$(System.DefaultWorkingDirectory)/Infracodetest-CI/Release1/s/VSTSDemoDeploy.json

Template parameters ⓘ
$(System.DefaultWorkingDirectory)/Infracodetest-CI/Release1/s/VSTSDemoParametersDev.json

Override template parameters ⓘ

Deployment mode *   ⓘ
Incremental

Figure 7-27. *Deployment configuration*

13. Save the settings. Add the next environment to the pipeline. Click the + below the existing environment (see Figure 7-28).

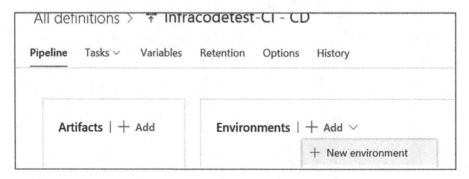

Figure 7-28. *Add new environment*

14. Enter the name of the new environment and the deployment tasks (as you did for the first environment). You can change the subscription/, resource group, location, and so forth, to differentiate it from the dev environment. Also, the parameter file should be selected per the target environment (see Figure 7-29).

Template *   ①

$(System.DefaultWorkingDirectory)/Infracodetest-CI/Release1/s/VSTSDemoDeploy.json

Template parameters ①

$(System.DefaultWorkingDirectory)/Infracodetest-CI/Release1/s/VSTSDemoParameterstest.json

Override template parameters ①

Figure 7-29. *Template configuration*

15. Save the changes to complete the release
     configuration (see Figure 7-30).

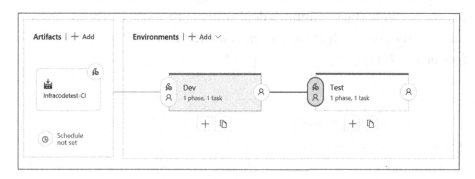

Figure 7-30. *Finalize release configuration*

16. If you click the environment's pre-deployment
     condition, you see that it is configured as
     autotriggered; for example, the test environment
     deployment is triggered once the dev environment
     deployment is completed. You can also choose to
     change it per your release process requirement
     (see Figure 7-31).

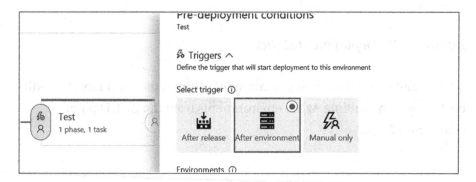

Figure 7-31. *Configure trigger*

Every time the code is committed in the source repository, the continuous integration trigger in the build config starts a build. The artifacts of this build include the JSON file and the target environment parameter files. The continuous deployment process is defined in the release process, which are autotriggered after the build has completed (see Figure 7-32).

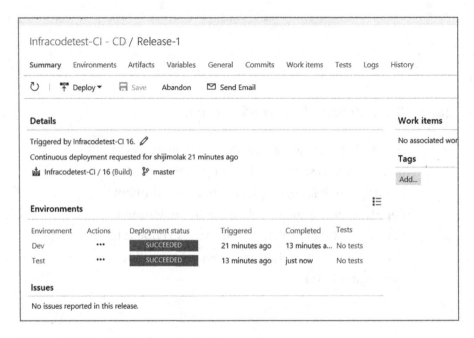

Figure 7-32. *Deployment status*

Depending on the target environment settings, the ARM template will be deployed in multiple Azure environments from the CI/CD pipeline (see Figure 7-33).

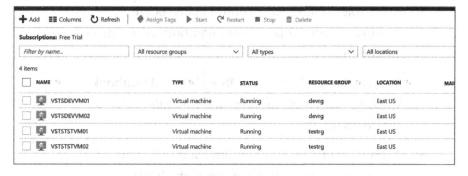

Figure 7-33. *Environment in Azure*

Azure Automation

Azure Automation is automation as a service offered from the Azure portal. It can be leveraged to automate platform-level tasks as well as on-premise environment. Azure Automation uses PowerShell and Python in the back end and supports the following types of runbooks:

- PowerShell

- PowerShell Workflow

- Graphical runbook

- Graphical PowerShell Workflow

- Python

Azure Automation features:

- It helps with process automation, configuration management, and update management.

- Automation accounts act as sandboxes and share resources available only to runbooks within the accounts.

- Azure role-based access control helps secure automation accounts against unauthorized access and execution.

- It can be integrated with OMS and Hybrid Runbook Worker to automate tasks in an on-premise environment.

- Azure Automation DSC (Desired State Configuration) is used for configuration management. It also ensures that a baseline config is maintained across environments.

With Azure Automation, you can create your own runbooks or select one from a list of runbooks in the gallery. The runbook gallery contains community-contributed runbooks, as well as the ones created by Microsoft (see Figure 7-34).

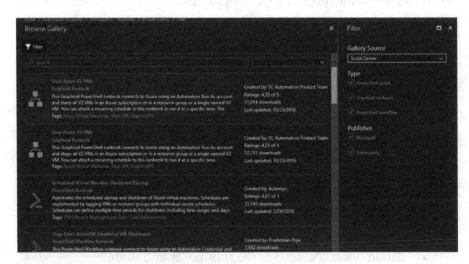

Figure 7-34. *Runbook gallery*

These runbooks cater to the majority of Azure IaaS use cases, including VM creation and management, disk encryption, key vault configuration, and so forth. It is recommended to leverage Azure Automation runbooks from the gallery wherever applicable to eliminate repeated manual tasks in the hosted environment.

Infrastructure Configuration Management

Azure Automation DSC uses PowerShell DSC and helps maintain a desired state configuration in environments hosted in Azure. It uses DSC Pull architecture where the connected VMs contact the hosted Azure Automation pull server to retrieve the latest configurations.

DSC configurations can be uploaded and compiled directly from the Azure portal.

1. **Navigate to Automation account ➤ Configuration management ➤ Add a configuration** to upload the DSC file. Once the file is uploaded, it can be complied to create the MOF file that is pulled and used by the Local Configuration Manager (LCM) of the target VMs (see Figure 7-35).

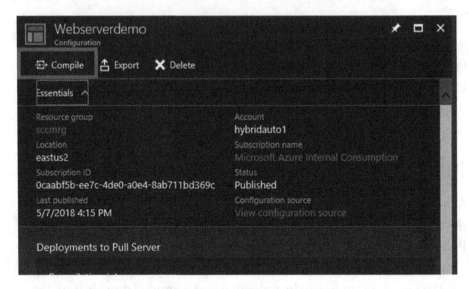

Figure 7-35. *Compile DSC configuration*

2. All the compiled DSC configurations can be viewed
    from the automation account at Configuration
    management ➤ DSC node configurations
    (see Figure 7-36).

Figure 7-36. *DSC compiled files*

3. It is easily to onboard Azure VMs to Azure
   Automation DSC. From the automation account,
   select **Configuration Management** ➤ **DSC nodes**
   ➤ **Add Azure VM** (see Figure 7-37).

Figure 7-37. *Add Azure VMs*

4. Select the VM and click **Connect** (see Figure 7-38).

Figure 7-38. *Connect VM*

5. Provide information for connecting the VM. Select the compiled DSC configuration file. Define the refresh frequency, during which the LCM contacts the Azure Automation DSC pull server. Define the configuration mode frequency, at which configuration is enforced. Define the configuration mode, which in this example is **ApplyAndMonitor**. If the configuration requires a reboot, the **Action after Reboot** should be selected (see Figure 7-39).

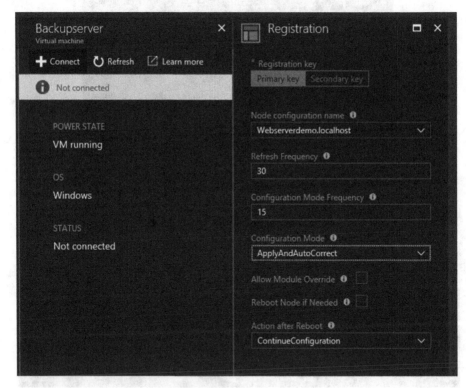

Figure 7-39. *DSC configuration*

6. The compliance status of all the VMs is monitored
    from the Azure portal. Select Automation account ➤
    Configuration Management ➤ DSC nodes
    (see Figure 7-40).

Figure 7-40. *DSC nodes*

Azure Automation DSC provides a single pane view of your Azure IaaS
environment compliance status against defined DSC configurations.

Integration with OMS

The Operations Management Suite (OMS) provides a centralized
management and monitoring solution for Azure IaaS environments. It
consists of four main pillars: log analytics, automation, backup, and site
recovery. Log analytics help you gain better insight into the underlying
infrastructure, which helps cloud administrators take preventive actions
against environment issues and to fine-tune resource performance.

The first step in leveraging log analytics is to create the workspace from
the Azure portal. Onboarding Azure virtual machines is simple because
they can be selected and linked directly to the workspace from the portal.

1. Select the workspace from Workspace Data Sources
    ➤ Virtual machines. This lists all the VMs in the
    subscription (see Figure 7-41).

Figure 7-41. *List of VMs that can be connected to OMS*

2. Select the VM that you wish to onboard and click
    Connect to link the VM to the OMS workspace.

Performance Metrics Monitoring

Windows and Linux performance counters can be configured at OMS
workspace ➤ Settings ➤ Data. Select **Windows Performance Counters**
and add the required performance counters (see Figure 7-42).

Figure 7-42. *Windows performance counters*

Follow the same process for Linux performance counters. Click **Save** to update the OMS workspace settings. Performance data is collected by OMS and can be analyzed to flag any performance bottlenecks.

Alerts and Auto Remediation

Performance metrics can be queried from OMS workspace ➤ Log search.

In the example shown in Figure 7-43, the logs are drilled down to "% Host Processor Usage" for a specific server.

Figure 7-43. *Log search*

Click **New Alert Rule** to create rules per the search results.

In the example shown in Figure 7-44, an alert generated is when there are more than five search results for a given criteria. OMS can be configured to autoremediate the alerts by initiating an automation runbook. The runbook is initiated by calling an automation runbook webhook URL. Alternatively, you can select the runbook from the automation account linked to the OMS workspace.

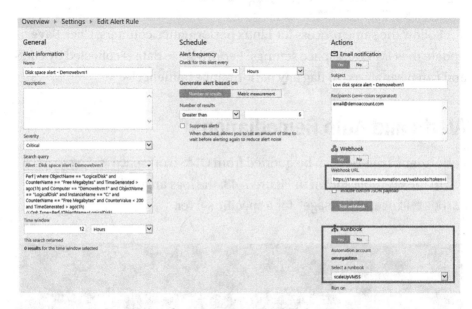

Figure 7-44. *Autoremediation using runbooks*

Summary

The Azure portal has many tools available for automating the provisioning and management of IaaS environments. These tools are leveraged mostly during the operational phase. Azure ARM helps with automation. OMS integrated with Azure Automation helps analyze and fine-tune the environment as defined by performance metrics.

CHAPTER 8

Practical Azure Security

When hosting applications in the cloud, security is a shared responsibility. While platform security is managed by Microsoft, it is up to the customers to adopt the many tools and services available in Azure to secure the hosted applications. The focal point here is to ensure confidentiality, integrity, and availability of customer data. This chapter focuses on some of the tools and services that should be incorporated in Azure IaaS architecture to ensure environment security.

Azure Resource Access Control

The most important design aspect of any architecture is defining the resource security boundaries. In Microsoft Azure, these boundaries are defined at different levels, the topmost being the subscription, followed by resource groups, and then the individual resources. Any permissions assigned at the top level are automatically inherited by the child resources.

© Shijimol Ambi Karthikeyan 2018
S. Ambi Karthikeyan, *Practical Microsoft Azure IaaS*,
https://doi.org/10.1007/978-1-4842-3763-2_8

Resource Group Segregation

Resource groups were introduced in the ARM model to help with the logical grouping of resources. For example, all resources in a specific environment—let's say DevTest or production—can be added to separate resource groups. Even though different subscriptions for different environments provide the highest level isolation, it may not be practically possible to manage and operate a large number of subscriptions. Hence, resource groups can be leveraged to group resources and manage them as a single entity. You can also extract the deployment details to an ARM template for redeploying the environment in the future. Any resources deployed in the ARM model should be part of a resource group. You can choose to use an existing resource group or to create a new resource group.

1. Search for "resource groups" in **All services**. Select the specific resource group to see all resources that are part of the group (see Figure 8-1).

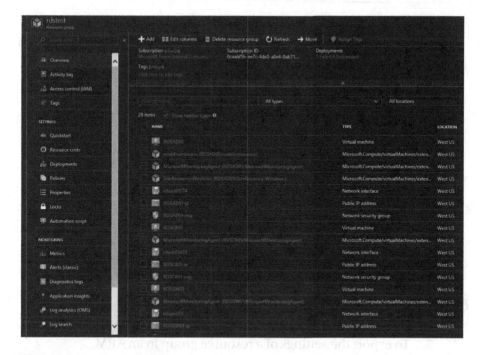

Figure 8-1. *Resource group*

It is interesting to note that when you create a VM inside a resource group, all associated components—like the NIC card, public IP address, and so forth—are created in the same resource group. When you delete the resource group, all resources in the resource group are deleted. This is very helpful from a management perspective for specific use cases. For example, you could include all resources for a test environment in a resource group and delete the resource group once testing is over.

2.   Click **+Add** if you want to add new resources to the group. Then select the type of resource you want to create or search for it. All available resource types are listed, and you can choose from the same (see Figure 8-2).

Figure 8-2. *Available resource types*

3. To export the settings of a resource group in an ARM
    template, select **Settings ➤ Automation script**
    (see Figure 8-3).

Figure 8-3. *Export ARM template*

You can choose to download the template, save it to the template library, or deploy it. Note that certain VM extensions, such as OMS and Azure Site Recovery agent, cannot be exported to a template. You might receive a warning message. The template export feature helps with redeployment of environments with the same specifications.

Role-Based Access Control

One of the important benefits of segregating environment-specific resources to a resource group is the ability to manage access control at the resource group level.

1. From the Resource group, click **Access Control (IAM)** to see information on all resources with access to the group (see Figure 8-4).

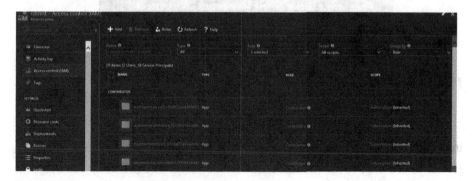

Figure 8-4. *Access control*

2. Click **Add** to give a new user access to the resource group. There are two aspects to adding permissions. First, select the role from the drop-down menu (see Figure 8-5).

235

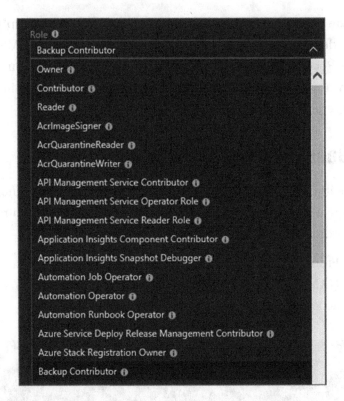

Figure 8-5. *Available roles*

You can see that there are a number of built-in roles already available in the list. Each of these roles has specific permissions associated with it. Hover your cursor over the information icon next to the role to see more details about the role. For example, choose the Automation Job Operator if you want to give permissions to a user to create and manage runbooks. Similarly, a Backup Reader role allows the user to simply view the status of backup services. In addition to the built-in roles, administrators can also create custom roles that allow only specific actions against defined resource types (see Figure 8-6).

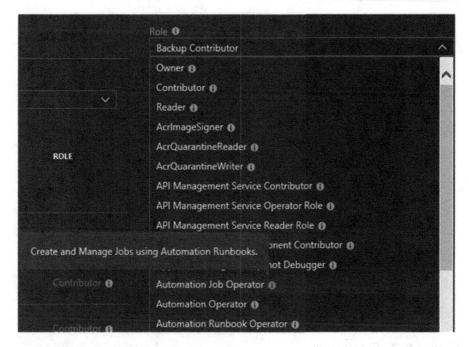

Figure 8-6. *Role description*

Search for the user with the username or email ID. You can either search for a user or group in Azure AD or search for a Microsoft ID. In the latter, an email is sent to the user with steps on how to get access to the resource (see Figure 8-7).

Figure 8-7. *Select user*

If you drill down to any of the resources in that resource group, you see that the permission is inherited from the resource (see Figure 8-8).

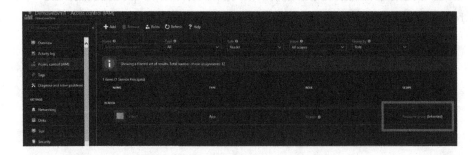

Figure 8-8. *Inherited permissions*

You can also provide access to users and groups at individual resource levels.

Resource Locks

Resource locks protect resources from accidental modification and deletion. Locks are implemented at subscription, resource group, or resource level. There are two types of locks available.

- **Read-only lock.** When implemented, this lock allows read-only access to the applied scope. Users are not able to delete or update any of the resources when the lock is applied to a resource group.

- **Delete lock**. This lock protects the resources from accidental deletion.

To configure resource locks, select the resource, **Settings ➤ Lock**. Click **Add**. Select the lock type, enter a lock name and notes, if any, and click **OK** (see Figure 8-9).

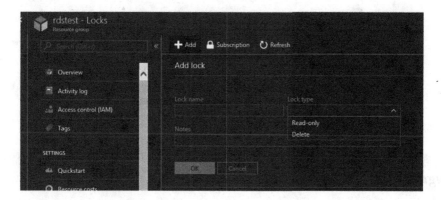

Figure 8-9. *Add locks*

When applied to a resource group, the locks are applicable to all the resources that are part of the group.

In Figure 8-10, a delete lock is applied to a resource group named rdstest.

239

Figure 8-10. *Delete lock*

When you try to delete a VM that is part of the resource group, it fails and shows the error message in Figure 8-11; thus, you can protect all of your resources in the resource group by applying a lock at the resource group level.

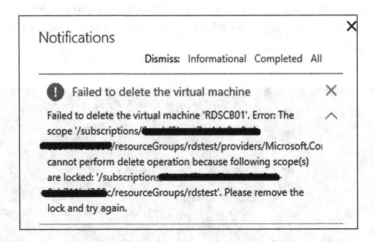

Figure 8-11. *Delete lock notification*

Access Audit

Azure activity logs provide insights into the administrative activities in your subscription. This is platform-level audit information. In order to get information at the OS level of VMs or network flows, additional log analytics and monitoring tools are required, which we discuss later in this chapter.

To view Azure platform logs, search for "activity log" in **All services** (see Figure 8-12).

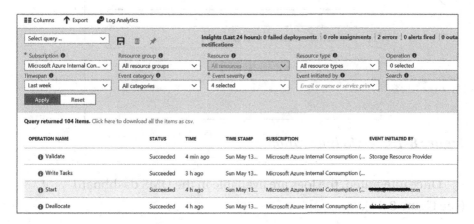

Figure 8-12. *Activity log*

Azure Activity Logs are integrated with log analytics for a detailed analysis of the data.

Click **Log analytics** above the logs. Click **+Add** in the next pane. Select the OMS workspace and the Azure subscription, the logs of which you want to integrate with the workspace (see Figure 8-13).

Figure 8-13. *OMS integration*

Once integrated, the logs are available in the OMS dashboard
(see Figure 8-14).

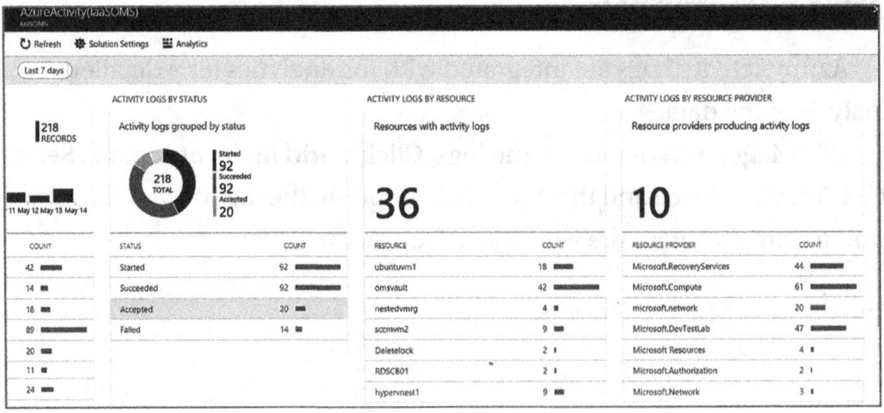

Figure 8-14. *Activity logs in the Azure dashboard*

You can leverage the log search and analysis capabilities available in OMS to get insights into Azure platform administration activities.

Azure VM Security

The security of a VM connected to a network can be ensured by tools and configurations at the network layer and the storage layer. The management plane security is managed by RBAC, as explained in the previous section. It determines who has access to the machine to make changes from the Azure portal. The thumb rule in all security configurations is to use the principle of least privilege: provide access only to those administrators or users who need access to VMs, and assign only the minimum required privileges to execute their tasks. The data plane security of VMs is linked to the controls implemented at the network and storage layers.

Azure Networking Security Boundaries

The various security layers offered in Azure are summarized in Figure 8-15.

Platform DDOS protection

Public IP

Virtual Network isolation and DDOS protection

NSG and UDR

Network Virtual Appliances

Azure Deployments

Figure 8-15. *Azure security layers*

The Azure virtual network in itself is a security boundary where VMs in one VNet are isolated from the VMs in other VNets by default unless communication is explicitly enabled by VPN connections or peerings. In addition, there are other security measures, such as NSGs, network virtual appliances, UDRs, and so forth, than can be leveraged to reinforce security.

DDoS Protection

Azure implements distributed denial-of-service (DDoS) protection, which protects the platform from targeted DDoS attacks. It is important to note that it is a platform-layer protection that cannot be configured by the user. In the event a DDoS attack is detected on an endpoint, the necessary actions are taken to confine the attack to the specific endpoint and not affect any other systems. This default protection mechanism is called

DDoS basic. There is a new DDoS protection called *DDoS standard* that was introduced to implement protection at the virtual network layer.

DDoS service for virtual networks can be enabled from **Virtual network ➤ Settings ➤ DDoS Protection**. Select the standard DDoS protection type. Select the DDoS protection plan (see Figure 8-16).

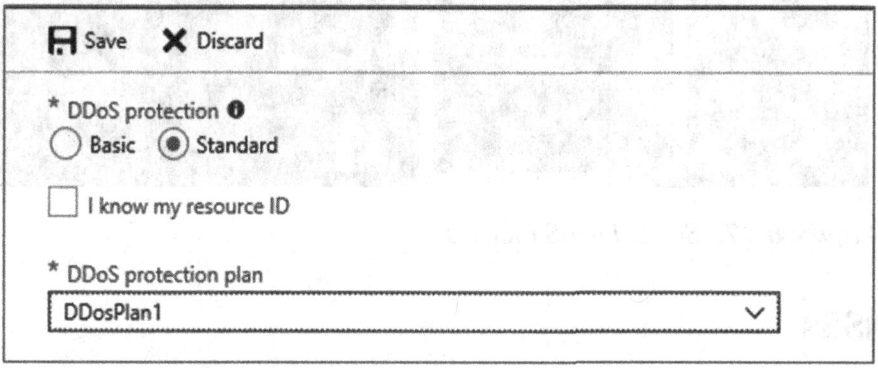

Figure 8-16. *Enabled DDoS protection*

DDoS Standard protects against volumetric-, protocol-, and application-layer attacks. Any resource that has a public IP associated with it is protected using DDoS Standard. You can select the DDoS metrics from the Azure monitor and configure it for alerts.

In **All services**, search for "monitor" to open the Azure Monitor dashboard. Select **Metrics** and choose the public IP address associated with the resource. The DDoS metrics are listed. You can choose the metrics you want to monitor and configure alerts (see Figure 8-17).

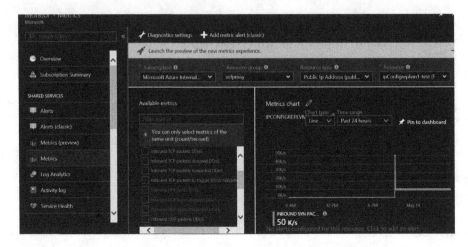

Figure 8-17. *Select DDoS metrics*

NSGs

Network security groups (NSGs) provide basic firewall-like functionalities in an Azure network and can be uses to filter the incoming and outgoing traffic from a virtual machine. NSGs are associated with either the NIC card of the VM (ARM model) or a subnet in a virtual network. When there are NSGs associated with both the subnet and the NIC card of the VM, the least permissive one takes precedence, depending on the flow of the traffic (i.e., either inbound or outbound).

Depending on the architecture being implemented, it is important to use NSGs to allow only legitimate traffic to reach the VMs. For example, in a three-tier architecture, you could restrict the DB tier to accept traffic only from the application tier.

1. From the Azure portal, search for "NSG" in
   All Services (see Figure 8-18).

Figure 8-18. *NSG*

2. Click **+Add** to create a new NSG. Provide the basic
    information, such as NSG name, resource group,
    and region to create the NSG (see Figure 8-19).

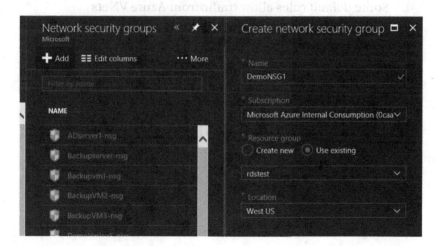

Figure 8-19. *Create NSG*

3. The two main settings in NSG are the inbound and
    outbound rules. To configure the inbound rule,
    select **Settings ➤ Inbound Security rules**
    (see Figure 8-20).

Figure 8-20. Inbound rules

4. Some default rules allow traffic from Azure VNets
    and load balancers. All other traffic is denied
    unless added explicitly. Click **+Add** to create a new
    inbound security rule (see Figure 8-21).

Figure 8-21. *Add rule*

- The source can be selected from the following options: Any, IP addresses, and Service tag. **Any** allows traffic from all sources. **IP addresses** restrict incoming traffic from a specific set of IP addresses or even a single IP when used with /32 CIDR. **Service tag** option s traffic from the Internet, virtual network, load balancer, and so forth. They are differentiated by the associated address space, depending on the selected tag.

- The source port, if known, can be specified.

- The destination can be selected from **Any**, **IP addresses**, or **Virtual network**. The destination port should be added to allow only traffic at a specific port. It is important to restrict all the values to implement the rule of least permission.

- Define the protocol, which is TCP, UDP or Any.

- Choose **Allow** or **Deny** from the Action menu items.

- Priority determines the order in which the rules are processed: the lower the number, the higher the priority.

- Provide a name to identity the rule and click **Add**.

Once created, the new rule is listed with the default rules (see Figure 8-22).

Figure 8-22. *New rule in NSG*

Outbound security rules are created in a similar manner; the only difference is in the logic where the rule is applied against outgoing traffic from the subnet/NIC card that it is associated to.

5. Associate the NSG with a NIC card or a subnet. From the NSG settings, select **Network interfaces** and click **Associate**. The network interfaces in the selected subscription and region are listed. You can choose the target NIC card and associate it with the NSG (see Figure 8-23).

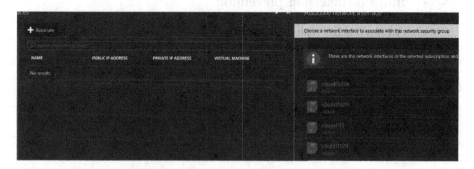

Figure 8-23. *Attach NIC card*

6. To associate a subnet with the NSG, go to **NSG settings ➤ Subnets** and click **+Associate**. Select the VNet and subnet from the region and click **OK** (see Figure 8-24).

Figure 8-24. *Attach Subnet*

Virtual Appliances

Network virtual appliances (NVAs) provide advanced functionalities when compared to the native security capabilities offered by NSGs and UDRs (user-defined routings). Virtual appliances enable the following security capabilities:

- Intrusion detection/prevention
- Advanced firewall and routing
- Vulnerability management and analysis
- Application protection and antivirus management
- Network traffic monitoring
- Network optimization

Many third-party vendors offer NVAs in the Azure Marketplace. These appliances can be purchased either on a pay-as-you-go model or with BYOL. The latter is useful in migration scenarios where organizations use network devices from third-party vendors and want to bring in the same capabilities in Azure. They can reuse the existing investments in these devices by deploying virtual appliances and leveraging the same licenses using the BYOL model.

Consider that an organization has existing investments in Cisco devices, such as firewall and WAN optimization devices, and wants to implement the same architecture in Azure. The organization can start by searching for Cisco appliances in the Azure Marketplace. All the available devices are listed with the type of licensing models. Select the device and proceed to deploy with the configuration (see Figure 8-25).

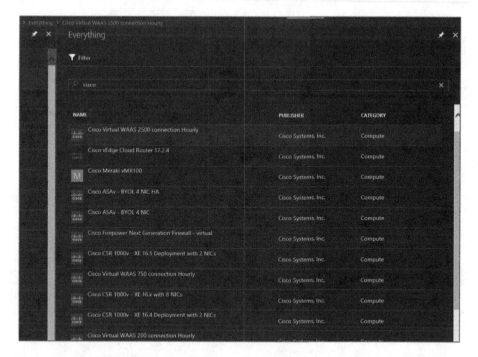

Figure 8-25. *Choose network virtual appliance*

Figure 8-26 is a sample architecture that uses a network virtual appliance.

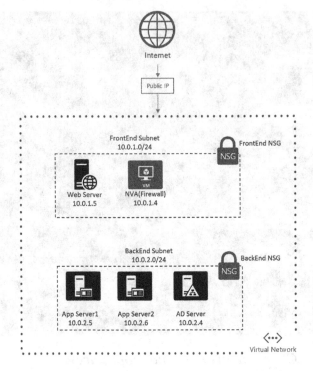

Figure 8-26. *Architecture using NSG*

Here a network appliance with advanced firewall capabilities is placed in the front-end subnet, and all incoming traffic traverses through this firewall.

Virtual Network Service Endpoints

VNet service endpoints restrict access to Azure Storage, SQL Database, Cosmos DB, and SQL Data Warehouse so that only traffic from a specific VNet is allowed to reach the resource. This helps enforce security posture in architectures where these resources are used. Azure VNet service endpoints have the following benefits:

- Access from public IP addresses is restricted and traffic is secured via VNet.

- Traffic via VNet traverses the Azure network backbone and helps optimize traffic when forced tunneling is used to send Internet-bound traffic via on-premise devices.

- Easy single-click configuration from the Azure management portal. It eliminates the need for reserving public IP addresses and firewalls to secure access to Azure resources.

To enable service endpoints, select the VNet and then **Settings ➤ Service Endpoints ➤ +Add**. Choose the service and the subnet for which you want to enable the service endpoints. In Figure 8-27, service endpoints are enabled for Azure SQL.

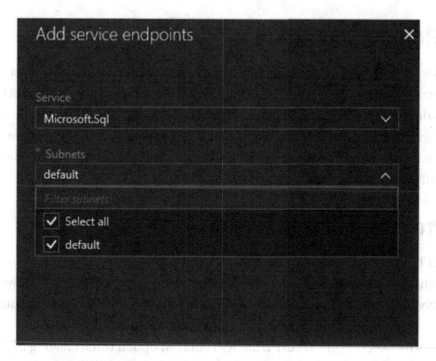

Figure 8-27. Select and enable service endpoint

255

It is important to note that enabling service endpoints alone is not enough. After enabling service endpoints for SQL, the network should be allowed access from the SQL Database firewall as well.

Forced Tunneling

Internet access is allowed by default from all Azure virtual networks. You could also restrict outbound traffic from VMs using NSGs. In some hybrid scenarios, it might be required to forward all Internet-bound traffic to on-premise for monitoring and analysis purposes as an additional security measure. This configuration is called *forced tunneling*, in which user-defined routes are implemented to send all Internet-bound traffic via the virtual network gateway.

Storage Security

The design of data-level security is as equally important as network layer security. Azure offers several mechanisms and tools to ensure the security of data at rest and data in motion. Azure IaaS VMs use Azure Storage to store virtual machine hard disks (VHDs). The options available to ensure security at the storage level are disk encryption, storage service encryption, and transport layer encryption.

Protecting Data in Motion

HTTPS protocol should be used for all REST APIs calls for data transmission over the Internet from Azure Storage. Azure file shares allow only SMB 3.0, which enables encrypted connections to on-premise clients. It is recommended to disable unencrypted data transfer at the storage level by selecting the **Secure transfer required** option when creating the storage account. It can also be configured after creating the storage from **Settings ➤ Configuration** (see Figure 8-28).

Figure 8-28. *Enforce secure transfer*

Disk Encryption Using Key Vault

Azure Disk Encryption is supported on both Windows and Linux VM using BitLocker and the DM-crypt feature, respectively. The keys used for encryption are stored in an Azure key Vault. This feature protects both existing and new VMs provisioned in Azure. If you are using pre-encrypted VHDs to create VMs, the encryption key should be uploaded to the key vault. The following are the prerequisites for Azure Disk Encryption:

- The key vault should be provisioned and available in the same region and subscription as the Azure VM.

- The EnabledForDiskEncryption setting should be enabled for the key vault so that the Azure platform can use the stored keys for volume encryption and decryption.

The easiest way to do this is by using the following Azure PowerShell command:

```
Set-AzureRmKeyVaultAccessPolicy -VaultName
<yourVaultName> -ResourceGroupName <yourResourceGroup>
-EnabledForDiskEncryption
```

1. Create an Application in Azure AD and generate a
    key to be used for key vault integration.

2. Give the AD application a wrap key and set
    permissions in the key vault. This can also be done
    using the following PowerShell code:

```
$keyVaultName = '<yourKeyVaultName>'
$aadClientID = '<yourAadAppClientID>'
$rgname = '<yourResourceGroup>'
Set-AzureRmKeyVaultAccessPolicy -VaultName $keyVaultName
-ServicePrincipalName $aadClientID -PermissionsToKeys 'WrapKey'
-PermissionsToSecrets 'Set' -ResourceGroupName $rgname
```

The Azure VM should be able to connect to Azure AD and key
vault endpoint for encryption. Ensure that there are no network layer
restrictions preventing this access.

You can use the following sample ARM template to create and encrypt
disks of a new VM.

```
{
    "$schema": "https://schema.management.azure.com/
    schemas/2015-01-01/deploymentTemplate.json#",
    "contentVersion": "1.0.0.0",
    "parameters": {
        "adminUsername": {
            "type": "String",
            "metadata": {
                "description": "Username for the Virtual Machine."
            }
        },
```

```
"adminPassword": {
    "type": "SecureString",
    "metadata": {
        "description": "Password for the Virtual Machine."
    }
},
"dnsLabelPrefix": {
    "type": "String",
    "metadata": {
        "description": "Unique DNS Name for the Public
            IP used to access the Virtual Machine."
    }
},
"windowsOSVersion": {
    "defaultValue": "2016-Datacenter",
    "allowedValues": [
        "2008-R2-SP1",
        "2012-Datacenter",
        "2012-R2-Datacenter",
        "2016-Nano-Server",
        "2016-Datacenter-with-Containers",
        "2016-Datacenter"
    ],
    "type": "String",
    "metadata": {
        "description": "The Windows version for the
            VM. This will pick a fully patched image of
            this given Windows version."
    }
},
```

```
"aadClientID": {
    "type": "string",
    "metadata": {
        "description": "Client ID of AAD app which has
            permissions to KeyVault"
    }
},
"aadClientSecret": {
    "type": "securestring",
    "metadata": {
        "description": "Client Secret of AAD app which
            has permissions to KeyVault"
    }
},
"keyVaultName": {
    "type": "string",
    "metadata": {
        "description": "Name of the KeyVault to place
            the volume encryption key"
    }
},
"keyVaultResourceGroup": {
    "type": "string",
    "metadata": {
        "description": "Resource group of the KeyVault"
    }
},
"useExistingKek": {
    "type": "string",
    "defaultValue": "nokek",
```

```
    "allowedValues": [
        "nokek",
        "kek"
    ],
    "metadata": {
        "description": "Select kek if the secret should
            be encrypted with a key encryption key and
            pass explicit keyEncryptionKeyURL. For nokek,
            you can keep keyEncryptionKeyURL empty."
    }
},
"keyEncryptionKeyURL": {
    "type": "string",
    "defaultValue": "",
    "metadata": {
        "description": "URL of the KeyEncryptionKey
            used to encrypt the volume encryption key"
    }
}
},
"variables": {
    "storageAccountName": "[concat(uniquestring(resource
        Group().id), 'sawinvm1')]",
    "nicName": "VMNic2",
    "addressPrefix": "10.3.0.0/16",
    "subnetName": "web",
    "subnetPrefix": "10.3.1.0/24",
    "publicIPAddressName": "PublicIPnew1",
    "vmName": "ARMWinVM",
    "virtualNetworkName": "holvnet1",
    "vmExtensionName": "dscExtension",
```

```
    "subnetRef": "[resourceId('Microsoft.Network/virtualNetworks/
    subnets', variables('virtualNetworkName'),
    variables('subnetName'))]"
},
"resources": [
    {
        "type": "Microsoft.Storage/storageAccounts",
        "sku": {
            "name": "Standard_LRS"
        },
        "kind": "Storage",
        "name": "[variables('storageAccountName')]",
        "apiVersion": "2016-01-01",
        "location": "[resourceGroup().location]",
        "properties": {}
    },
    {
        "type": "Microsoft.Network/publicIPAddresses",
        "name": "[variables('publicIPAddressName')]",
        "apiVersion": "2016-03-30",
        "location": "[resourceGroup().location]",
        "properties": {
            "publicIPAllocationMethod": "Dynamic",
            "dnsSettings": {
                "domainNameLabel": "[parameters('dnsLabel
                Prefix')]"
            }
        }
    },
    {
        "type": "Microsoft.Network/networkInterfaces",
```

```
    "name": "[variables('nicName')]",
    "apiVersion": "2016-03-30",
    "location": "[resourceGroup().location]",
    "properties": {
        "ipConfigurations": [
            {
                "name": "ipconfig1",
                "properties": {
                    "privateIPAllocationMethod": "Dynamic",
                    "publicIPAddress": {
                        "id": "[resourceId('Microsoft.
                        Network/publicIPAddresses',
                        variables('publicIPAddress
                        Name'))]"
                    },
                    "subnet": {
                        "id": "[variables('subnetRef')]"
                    }
                }
            }
        ]
    },
    "dependsOn": [

        "[resourceId('Microsoft.Network/publicIPAddresses/',
        variables('publicIPAddressName'))]"
    ]
},
{

    "type": "Microsoft.Compute/virtualMachines",
    "name": "[variables('vmName')]",
    "apiVersion": "2017-03-30",
```

```
        "location": "[resourceGroup().location]",
        "properties": {
            "hardwareProfile": {
                "vmSize": "Standard_A2"
            },
            "osProfile": {
                "computerName": "[variables('vmName')]",
                "adminUsername": "[parameters('adminUsername')]",
                "adminPassword": "[parameters('adminPassword')]"
            },
            "storageProfile": {
                "imageReference": {
                    "publisher": "MicrosoftWindowsServer",
                    "offer": "WindowsServer",
                    "sku": "[parameters('windowsOSVersion')]",
                    "version": "latest"
                },
                "osDisk": {
                    "createOption": "FromImage"
                },
                "dataDisks": [
                    {
                        "diskSizeGB": 1023,
                        "lun": 0,
                        "createOption": "Empty"
                    }
                ]
            },
            "networkProfile": {
                "networkInterfaces": [
                    {
```

```
                "id": "[resourceId('Microsoft.
                Network/networkInterfaces',
                variables('nicName'))]"
            }
        ]
    },
    "diagnosticsProfile": {
        "bootDiagnostics": {
            "enabled": true,
            "storageUri": "[reference(resourceId('
            Microsoft.Storage/storageAccounts/',
            variables('storageAccountName'))).
            primaryEndpoints.blob]"
        }
    }
},
"dependsOn": [
    "[resourceId('Microsoft.Storage/storageAccounts/',
    variables('storageAccountName'))]",

    "[resourceId('Microsoft.Network/networkInterfaces/',
    variables('nicName'))]"
]
},
{
    "name": "UpdateEncryptionSettings",
    "type": "Microsoft.Resources/deployments",
    "apiVersion": "2015-01-01",
    "dependsOn": [
        "[concat('Microsoft.Compute/virtualMachines/',
        variables('vmName'))]"
    ],
```

```
"properties": {
    "mode": "Incremental",
    "templateLink": {
        "uri": "https://raw.githubusercontent.
        com/Azure/azure-quickstart-templates/
        master/201-encrypt-running-windows-vm/
        azuredeploy.json",
        "contentVersion": "1.0.0.0"
    },
    "parameters": {
        "vmName": {
            "value": "[variables('vmName')]"
        },
        "aadClientID": {
            "value": "[parameters('aadClientID')]"
        },
        "aadClientSecret": {
            "value": "[parameters('aadClientSecret')]"
        },
        "keyVaultName": {
            "value": "[parameters('keyVaultName')]"
        },
        "keyVaultResourceGroup": {
            "value": "[parameters('keyVaultResourceGroup')]"
        },
        "useExistingKek": {
            "value": "[parameters('useExistingKek')]"
        },
        "keyEncryptionKeyURL": {
            "value": "[parameters('keyEncryption
            KeyURL')]"
```

```
                }
              }
            }
          }
        ],
        "outputs": {
            "hostname": {
                "type": "String",
                "value": "[reference(variables('publicIPAddress
                Name')).dnsSettings.fqdn]"
            }
        }
    }
}
```

Storage Service Encryption

The encryption of storage is now enabled by default for all Azure storages. Encryption is done using Microsoft managed keys, which uses 256-bit AES encryption to ensure the security of data at rest. There is no additional configuration required from the user side to enable it. Encryption using customer managed keys is also supported, and the key used for encryption is stored in an Azure key vault. To configure encryption using customer managed keys, select **settings ➤ Encryption**. Enable the **Use your own key** checkbox. Choose either **Enter key URI** or **Select from Key Vault** (see Figure 8-29).

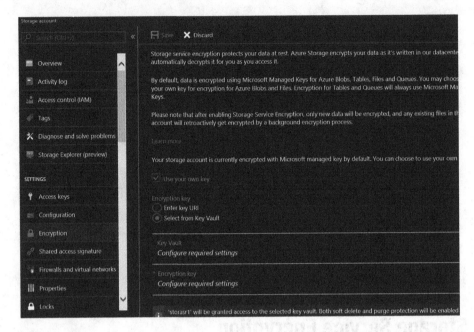

Figure 8-29. *Storage service encryption using consumer managed keys*

OMS Security Solutions

The Operations Management Suite (OMS) is built with a number of security solutions that provide insights into Azure IaaS security posture. You can follow the instructions in Chapter 7 to onboard Azure virtual machines to OMS. Once onboarded, enable the security solutions available in OMS to analyze the environment for any security breaches or threats.

From the OMS portal solutions gallery, select **Security & Compliance** and click **Add** (see Figure 8-30).

Figure 8-30. *Adds solution*

You should be able to see the **Antimalware Assessment** and **Security and Audit** solutions in the OMS home page after a few minutes.

The security and audit solution provides a dashboard view of the environment security status (see Figure 8-31).

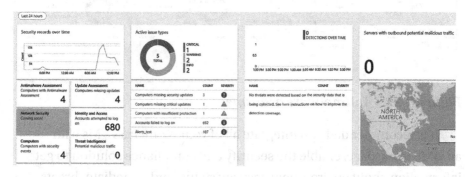

Figure 8-31. *Security and audit dashboard*

Issues such as missing updates and network threats, if any, are highlighted in the dashboard. You can drill down into each of the findings to get more insights. For example, you can click the missing security updates findings to understand the affected systems (see Figure 8-32).

Figure 8-32. *Missing updates sample*

The antimalware assessment solution can be navigated from the same dashboard. You can see the status of antimalware protection and computers with insufficient protection, and drill down deeper to get more information about affected servers (see Figure 8-33).

Figure 8-33. *Antimalware assessment*

It is recommended you integrate all of your Azure IaaS VMs with an OMS workspace, enable the security and compliance solution to get information about environment security status, and remediate threats.

Azure Security Center

The Azure Security Center analyzes your Azure environment against best practices and possible security threats. The security center has evolved to provide the same services to on-premise workloads if they are connected to an OMS workspace in the subscription. The connected systems are analyzed against defined policies for Azure deployment best practices. They are also analyzed against security baselines. The gaps are highlighted and actionable recommendations are offered. The free tier of Azure Security center is enabled by default for all Azure subscriptions and associated resources. If you want to use advanced features such as just-in-time (JIT) VM access, adaptive application controls, and advanced threat detection, you must upgrade to the paid version (i.e., the standard tier).

The security polices for the security center can be viewed at and modified from **Security Center ➤ Security Policy ➤ Select Subscription ➤ Security Policy**. You can enable or disable the recommendations to fine-tune the data displayed in the security center (see Figure 8-34).

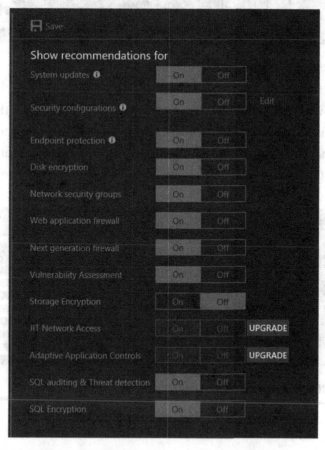

***Figure 8-34.** Security center policy configuration*

The Overview tab provides itemized information on the status of compute, networking, storage, and data and applications (see Figure 8-35).

Figure 8-35. *Security center dashboard*

Drill down to each resource type to understand more about the critical items flagged in the dashboard. For example, the compute status highlights potential issues with endpoint protection, missing scan data, missing system updates, restart pending, and so forth (see Figure 8-36).

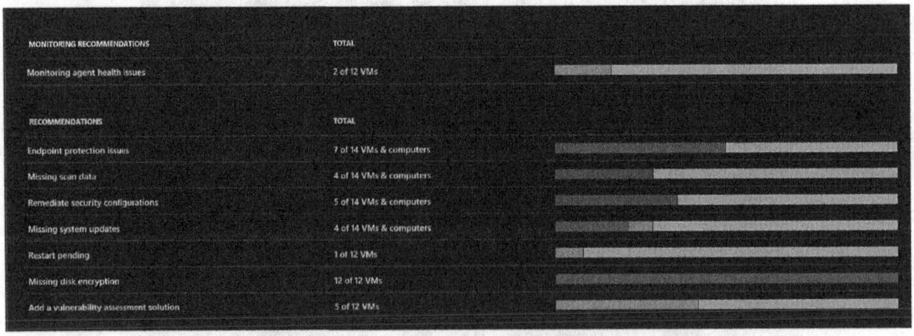

Figure 8-36. *Compute recommendations*

You can drill down to get more information on each item. The status of VMs against security baselines is seen in Figure 8-37.

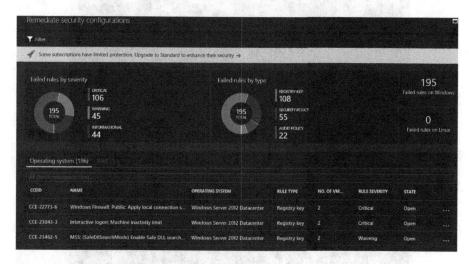

Figure 8-37. *Security baseline analysis*

Click each of the recommendations to view further details on the CCEID and the proposed remediation steps. A sample is shown in Figure 8-38.

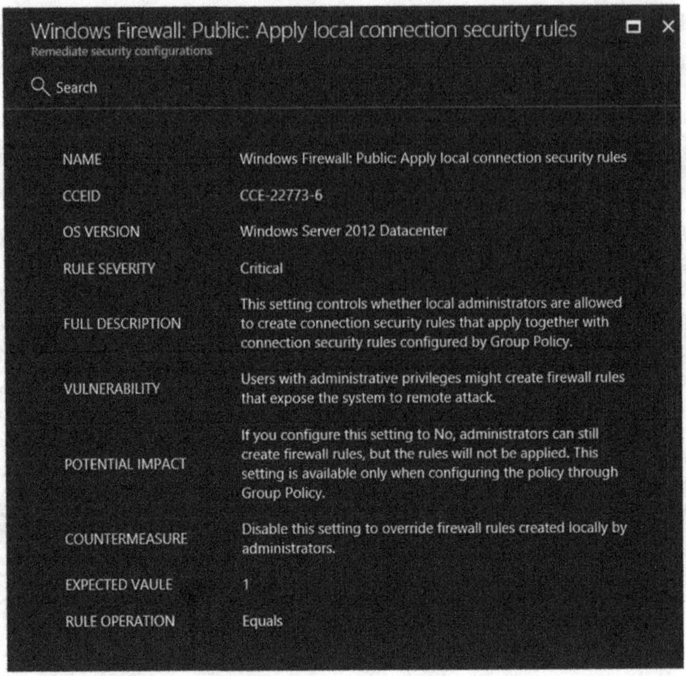

Figure 8-38. Sample recommendation

For some of the recommendations, remediation is done directly from the security center. Consider the recommendation shown in Figure 8-39 that highlights missing NSGs on a VM.

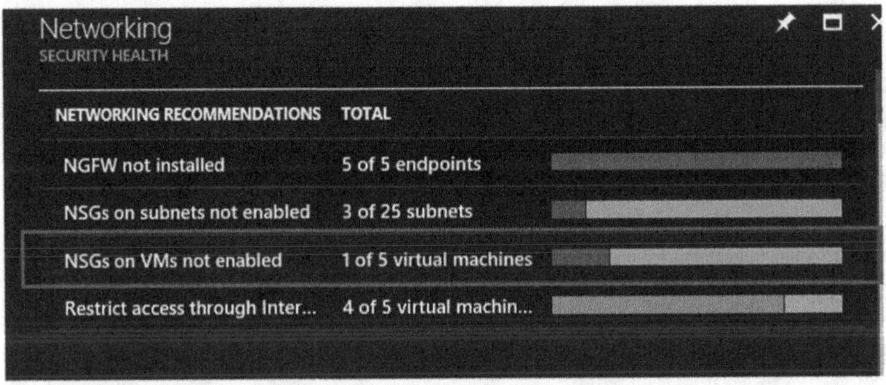

Figure 8-39. Network baseline recommendation

The VM with missing a NSG is highlighted and you get an option to create and attach and NSG to remediate the issue (see Figure 8-40).

Figure 8-40. *Network baseline remediation*

Summary

Security should be built into Azure architecture from the ground up and cover compute, storage, and network components. Along with built-in tools and features such as NSG, VNet service endpoints, disk encryption, OMS, and security centers, third-party virtual appliances can also be used to ensure the security of hosted environments.

CHAPTER 9

Common IaaS Architectures and Implementation Guidelines

The major IaaS design principles and guidelines were covered in the previous chapters. Any architecture—from inception phase to implementation phase—should be analyzed for adherence to these principles. Building a scalable, resilient, highly available, and secure environment requires meticulous planning and design. This chapter covers some of the common IaaS architectures and includes practical scenarios faced by organizations adopting Azure or building a hybrid cloud environment that leverages Azure.

Extending On-Premise Active Directory to Azure

Many organizations go through a phase of coexistence when adopting Azure, where part of their resources exist on-premise and part of them are migrated to the cloud. Extending the identity service to Azure is

© Shijimol Ambi Karthikeyan 2018
S. Ambi Karthikeyan, *Practical Microsoft Azure IaaS*,
https://doi.org/10.1007/978-1-4842-3763-2_9

an important milestone in this phase. The applications deployed in Azure require access to the on-premise domain for authentication and authorization purposes.

The very first step in this architecture is to establish the network connectivity to Azure VNet via ExpressRoute or VPN. ExpressRoute is the recommended option for stable, redundant connectivity with assured bandwidth. Alternatively, organizations can choose Site-to-Site VPN if they want a more economical option or if they don't have ExpressRoute connectivity available closer to their datacenter region. The architecture shown in Figure 9-1 uses Site-to-Site VPN connectivity from on-premise to Azure. The premise is to extend the same Active Directory (AD) domain to the VNet in Azure, where additional application servers will be deployed.

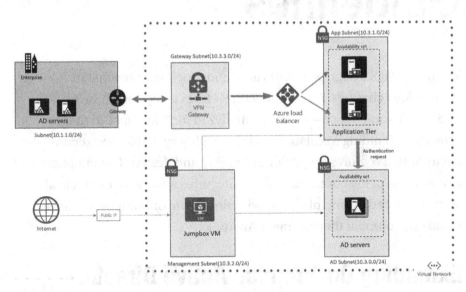

Figure 9-1. *Extend on-premise AD to Azure*

Implementation Guidelines

The following are prerequisites.

- The on-premise network should have a perimeter device that supports an Azure Site-to-Site VPN over IPsec/IKE (IKE v1 or v2). Microsoft publishes a list of supported VPN devices and configuration scripts that can be used for on-premise device configuration. Devices other than the published ones can also be used if the VPN protocols are supported.

- There should be a free, public IP available at the on-premise network assigned to the gateway to connect to the network.

- When the Azure VNet is designed, ensure that there is no IP address range overlap with the on-premise network.

VPN Setup

Once the virtual network is configured in Azure, the next step is to create a gateway subnet. This is a prerequisite for creating the virtual network gateway.

1. The gateway subnet can be created from VNet ➤ settings ➤ **Subnets**. Click +**Gateway subnet** (see Figure 9-2).

Figure 9-2. *Add gateway subnet*

2. You can change the gateway subnet IP range if
    required, but note that the network name cannot be
    changed (see Figure 9-3).

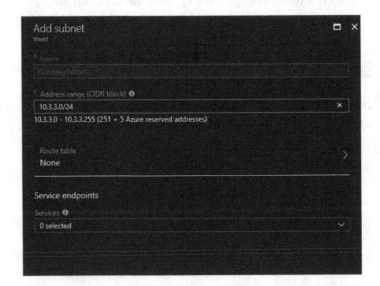

Figure 9-3. *Gateway subnet details*

Note that the name of the subnet cannot be edited. If necessary, the address range can be edited.

3. Search for the virtual network gateway from **All services**.

4. Create a new gateway (see Figure 9-4).

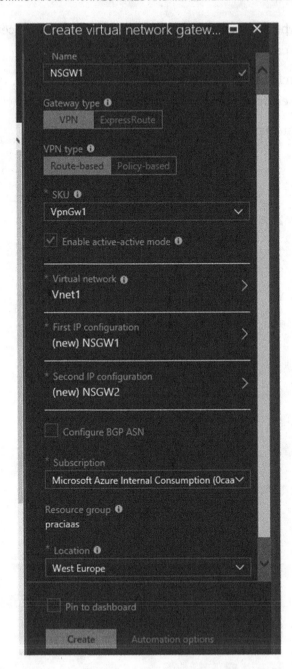

Figure 9-4. *Create a new virtual network gateway*

5. There are two types of gateways available: VPN and ExpressRoute. Select the VPN gateway.

    •   The VPN type us either route based or policy based. Policy-based VPNs work on static routing. Route-based VPNs allow dynamic routing. If you want to connect multiple networks to the same gateway, choose route based.

    •   Select **Enable active-active mode** to configure the gateway for high availability.

    •   Select the virtual network with the gateway subnet and create two public IP addresses for the gateway (since we are using active-active HA configuration).

6. The gateway could take up to 45 minutes to provision. To configure the Site-to-Site connection, select **Gateway ➤ Settings ➤ Connections**. Click **+Add** (see Figure 9-5).

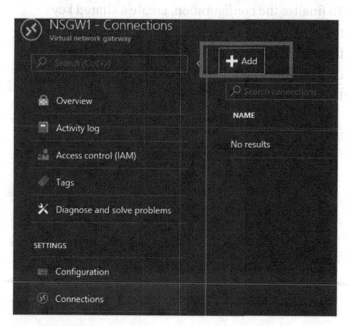

Figure 9-5. Add connection

7. While configuring the Site-to-Site connection, you should create a local network gateway by providing the on-premise device public IP and the datacenter private IP range allowed to communicate over the VPN (see Figure 9-6).

Figure 9-6. *Local network gateway connection*

8. To finalize the configuration, create a shared key that will be used by the on-premise device and to encrypt the connection. This key should be a combination of numbers and letters (encrypted format), as shown in Figure 9-7.

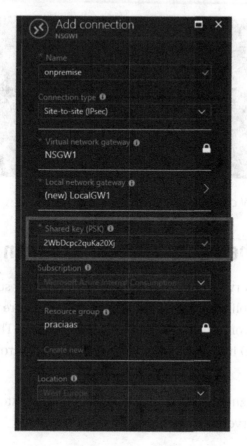

Figure 9-7. *Shared key configuration*

A **Connected** status indicates that the Azure VPN gateway was able to establish a VPN connection with on-premise (see Figure 9-8).

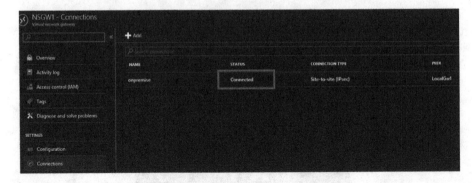

Figure 9-8. *VPN connection status*

Configure the Azure VNet for Extending Domain

The Active Directory VMs are deployed in an availability set in the AD subnet. After establishing the VPN connectivity, configure the VNet's DNS to point to the on-premise AD server private IP address. This is required to promote the AD in Azure as a secondary domain controller of the on-premise domain.

1. Go to Azure VNet settings ➤ DNS. Add the custom DNS server IP address (see Figure 9-9).

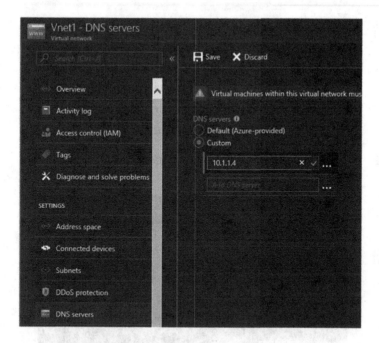

Figure 9-9. *Customer DNS*

2. Before proceeding with the AD promotion, make
    sure that the on-premise domain is being resolved
    (see Figure 9-10).

```
10.3.0.4 - Remote Desktop Connection

C:\Users\Azureuser> ping demolabscloud.com

nging demolabscloud.com [10.1.1.4] with 32 bytes of data:
ply from 10.1.1.4: bytes=32 time=157ms TTL=126
ply from 10.1.1.4: bytes=32 time=156ms TTL=126
ply from 10.1.1.4: bytes=32 time=157ms TTL=126
ply from 10.1.1.4: bytes=32 time=158ms TTL=126

ng statistics for 10.1.1.4:
    Packets: Sent = 4, Received = 4, Lost = 0 (0% loss),
proximate round trip times in milli-seconds:
    Minimum = 156ms, Maximum = 158ms, Average = 157ms
C:\Users\Azureuser> _
```

Figure 9-10. *Domain name resolution from Azure*

3. Configure the machine's IP as static from the NIC card settings. This ensures that the IP is not released to any other VMs when the machine is restarted or stopped from the Azure portal. From the virtual machine settings, select **Networking** ➤ <network interface of the VM> ➤ **Settings** ➤ **IP configurations**.

4. Set the private IP as static (see Figure 9-11).

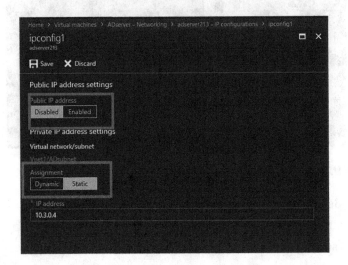

Figure 9-11. *AD VM IP configuration*

As part of security best practice, the public IP can also be disabled. Since the VPN connection is already established, you should be able to connect to this VM from your on-premise network using the private IP. The public IP is enabled on the Jumpbox VM in the network, which can be used to connect to the other VMs in the VNet.

Now we can proceed to promote this server as a secondary AD of the on-premise domain. After promoting the machine as AD, you can change the VNet's DNS settings to use the new AD server so that the DNS traffic is not redirected to on-premise. The on-premise AD can still be added as the secondary DNS in custom settings for redundancy (see Figure 9-12).

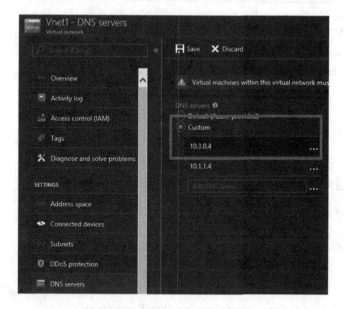

Figure 9-12. *Add the IP of AD hosted in Azure*

It is also recommended to create sites and subnets in Active Directory for on-prem and Azure networks. The AD servers associated with each subnet can be moved to the corresponding sites. With respect to the AD operations master's role, it is recommended to restrict the roles to AD servers hosted on-premise (see Figure 9-13).

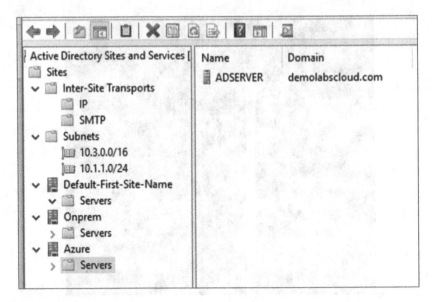

Figure 9-13. *AD Sites and Services configuration*

Note   The implementation steps for other major components in this architecture (i.e., Azure load balancers and network security groups) were covered in Chapters 6 and 8, respectively.

Network Hub and Spoke Topology

Workloads can be separated into different virtual networks in Azure; however, in some scenarios, you may need to connect these VNets to a central VNet that has connectivity to the on-premise network. This architecture is called *hub and spoke* topology, with the central VNet acting as the hub, and the other connected VNets acting as spokes (see Figure 9-14).

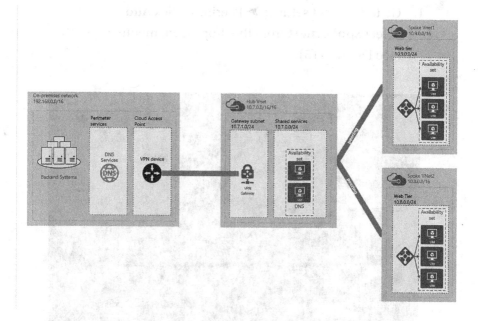

Figure 9-14. *Network hub and spoke topology*

Prerequisites

The prerequisites discussed in the previous architecture are also applicable here for establishing VPN connectivity to the hub VNet to on-premise. And, there shouldn't be any IP overlap between the VNets that are peered.

VNet Peering Configuration

The first step is to establish VPN connectivity from hub VNet to on-premise. The steps for configuring Site-to-Site VPNs are covered in the previous architecture implementation guidelines. VNet peering should be configured from the hub VNet to both spoke VNet 1 and spoke VNet 2. Note that we do not need a gateway to establish this connection, and hence it is more economical. Also, all the traffic in the peered connection traverses through the Azure backbone.

1. Go to Hubvnet settings ➤ Peerings. Click **Add**.
   Select **Spokevnet1** from the drop-down menu
   (see Figure 9-15).

Figure 9-15. *Peering configuration*

2. Add Spokevnet2 as was done in step 1.

3. In Spokevnet1 and Spokevnet2, add a peering
   connection to Hubvnet. Once these connections are
   created, the status of peering is shown as connected
   in Hubvnet (see Figure 9-16).

Figure 9-16. Peering status

Once the peering connection is established, the resources connected in the spoke VNets can communicate with hub VNets and vice versa. Hub VNets usually have common services such as AD or file shares accessed by resources in a spoke VNet as well as from on-premise.

The N-tier Application in Azure

There are several variations of architectures available for N-Tier application deployment in Azure. In this sample reference architecture, there are three tiers: web tier, application tier, and DB tier. VNet service endpoints are used to secure access to the Azure SQL Database used in the DB tier (see Figure 9-17).

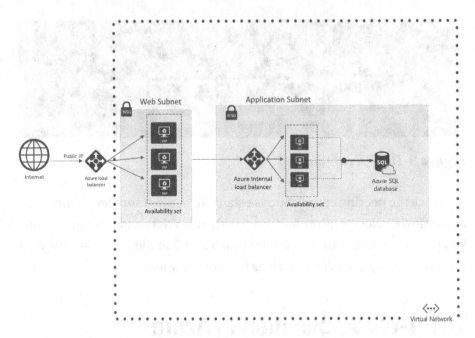

Figure 9-17. N-tier application in Azure

Access to the web tier is through a public load balancer. Application tier VMs have an internal load balancer that accepts traffic coming from the web tier. Network system groups (NSGs) should be implemented to allow only least permissive inbound and outbound traffic, as per the application requirement.

The additional component in this architecture is the VNet service endpoint configuration.

1. To enable service endpoints, select the VNet ➤ settings ➤ **Service endpoints** ➤ **+Add**. Choose **Microsoft.SQL** as the service and **AppSubnet** as the subnet. The service endpoint is listed in the VNet settings (see Figure 9-18).

Figure 9-18.   *VNet service endpoints*

2. Configure SQL Database to allow access from the
    subnet. Select the Azure SQL server ➤ **Security** ➤
    Firewalls and virtual networks. Click **Add existing
    virtual network** (see Figure 9-19).

Figure 9-19.   *SQL DB firewall configuration*

3. Select the virtual network and app subnet
    (see Figure 9-20).

Figure 9-20.   Select VNet and app subnet

4. Once the rule is created and the status becomes
Ready, the VMs in app subnet can connect to the DB
over the Azure network backbone (see Figure 9-21).

Figure 9-21.   VNet service endpoint status

Other Reference Architectures

The Azure Architecture Center (https://docs.microsoft.com/en-us/
azure/architecture/) provides comprehensive reference architecture for
multiple use cases.

Two of the most common IaaS architectures from the Azure
Architecture Center are replicated in the next section for reference.

Multiregion N-tier Application

In this architecture, the applications are deployed in two Azure regions for higher availability and disaster recovery (see Figure 9-22).

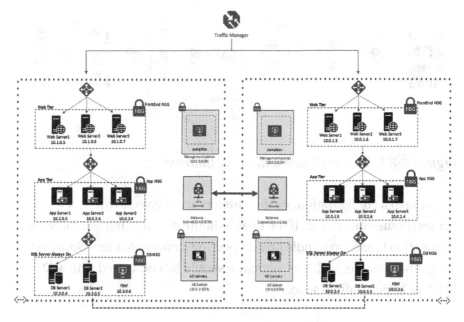

Figure 9-22. *Multiregion N-tier application*

Azure Traffic Manager routes the application to the primary region. If the primary region becomes unavailable, the traffic is redirected to a secondary region. SQL Server Always On Client Connectivity is used for resiliency at the database layer and requires network connectivity between regions. In this architecture, it is achieved using a VPN connection. Alternatively, VNet peering can be used to establish the connectivity.

ExpressRoute with VPN failover

In this architecture, the ExpressRoute connection coexists with the VPN connection to the Azure Virtual Network (see Figure 9-23).

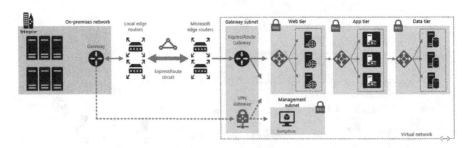

Figure 9-23. *ExpressRoute with VPN failover*

In such a configuration, the first preference is given to the ExpressRoute connection. If the ExpressRoute circuit fails, then the VPN connection is used to handle private peering communication. Note that the gateway subnet in this architecture should be configured with a /27 CIDR or larger address space.

Summary

This chapter have reviewed some IaaS architectures and their implementation aspects. Many of the Azure IaaS prominent features discussed in previous chapters are reflected in these architectures; for example, the combination of availability sets and load balancers is found in all architectures to ensure high availability, and NSGs are used to implement least-privileged network access. Depending on the use case, the right tools and best practices should be adopted to implement a scalable, highly available, and secure architecture in Azure.

Index

© Shijimol Ambi Karthikeyan 2018
S. Ambi Karthikeyan, *Practical Microsoft Azure IaaS*,
https://doi.org/10.1007/978-1-4842-3763-2

Printed in the United States
By Bookmasters